Cambridge Elements ≡

Elements in Critical Heritage Studies
edited by
Kristian Kristiansen, *University of Gothenburg*
Michael Rowlands, *UCL*
Francis Nyamnjoh, *University of Cape Town*
Astrid Swenson, *Bath University*
Shu-Li Wang, *Academia Sinica*
Ola Wetterberg, *University of Gothenburg*

HERITAGE MAKING AND MIGRANT SUBJECTS IN THE DEINDUSTRIALISING REGION OF THE LATROBE VALLEY

Alexandra Dellios
Australian National University

CAMBRIDGE
UNIVERSITY PRESS

CAMBRIDGE
UNIVERSITY PRESS

University Printing House, Cambridge CB2 8BS, United Kingdom

One Liberty Plaza, 20th Floor, New York, NY 10006, USA

477 Williamstown Road, Port Melbourne, VIC 3207, Australia

314–321, 3rd Floor, Plot 3, Splendor Forum, Jasola District Centre,
New Delhi – 110025, India

103 Penang Road, #05–06/07, Visioncrest Commercial, Singapore 238467

Cambridge University Press is part of the University of Cambridge.

It furthers the University's mission by disseminating knowledge in the pursuit of
education, learning, and research at the highest international levels of excellence.

www.cambridge.org
Information on this title: www.cambridge.org/9781108826495
DOI: 10.1017/9781108919937

First published 2022

A catalogue record for this publication is available from the British Library.

ISBN 978-1-108-82649-5 Paperback
ISSN 2632-7074 (online)
ISSN 2632-7066 (print)

Heritage Making and Migrant Subjects in the Deindustrialising Region of the Latrobe Valley

Elements in Critical Heritage Studies

DOI: 10.1017/9781108919937
First published online: March 2022

Alexandra Dellios
Australian National University

Author for correspondence: Alexandra Dellios, alexandra.dellios@anu.edu.au

Abstract: This Element argues that community-initiated migrant heritage harbours the potential to challenge and expand state-sanctioned renderings of multiculturalism in liberal nation states. In this search for alternative readings, community-initiated migrant heritage is positioned as a grassroots challenge to positivist state multiculturalism. It can do this if we adopt the migrant perspective, a diasporic perspective of 'settlement' that is always unfinished, non-static, and non-essentialist. As mobile subjects, either once or many times over – a subject position arrived at through acts of mobility, sometimes spawned by violence or structural inequality, which can reverberate throughout subsequent generations – the migrant subject position compels us to look both forwards and backwards in time and place.

Keywords: migrant, industrial, heritage, memory, emotion

ISBNs: 9781108826495 (PB), 9781108919937 (OC)
ISSNs: 2632-7074 (online), 2632-7066 (print)

Contents

Introduction

In March 2007, in the small deindustrialising town of Morwell in Australia's south-east, a local group with a post-WWII migrant background launched a public park. In itself, this was not a unique occurrence. The region is dotted with public parks. But this space is unique: the Gippsland Immigration Park was conceived, designed, launched, and managed by locals who seek to commemorate, memorialise, and celebrate migrants and migration to the region of Gippsland and the Latrobe Valley. In Australia's largely Anglophone heritage landscape, such a community-initiated migrant heritage space warrants attention. As a multiform, open-air space, the Park is a platform etched with many contested and intertwined histories: it engages directly with circulating narratives around industrialisation, migration, and working lives. And it was created in a context familiar to many Western immigrant-receiving nations: in the wake of the privatisation of primary industries and widespread unemployment. As the former coal-fired powerhouse of the state of Victoria and a magnet for migrant workers, the Latrobe Valley was acutely affected by socio-economic changes from the late 1980s. The Park therefore presents a unique opportunity to explore migrant subjectivities in the context of historical change. Given the contradictions of recent politics in self-proclaimed multicultural nation states – and a heated identity politics that draws on essentialist notions of race and ethnicity – as researchers, it is our task to interrogate the spaces and structures that exist for migrant community groups to voice their own histories of immigration and settlement. How do communities remember migrant labour in post-industrial places? The case study of the Gippsland Immigration Park offers a means to unpack the Latrobe Valley's recent industrial and post-industrial history and to examine the shared and layered community histories of that place in a liberal multicultural nation state. This is both a migrant and an industrial history.

This Element argues that community-initiated migrant heritage harbours the potential to challenge and expand state-sanctioned renderings of multiculturalism in liberal nation states. In this search for alternative readings, community-initiated migrant heritage is positioned as a grassroots challenge to positivist state multiculturalism. It can do this if we adopt the migrant perspective, a diasporic perspective of 'settlement' that is always unfinished, non-static, and non-essentialist. As mobile subjects, either once or many times over – a subject position arrived at through acts of mobility, sometimes spawned by violence or structural inequality, which can reverberate throughout subsequent generations – the migrant subject position compels us to look both forwards and backwards in time and place. This is a perspective that can also be mirrored in the migrant subject's approach to heritage and memory, which are similarly

Figure 1 Gippsland Immigration Park, in Morwell, VIC (photo taken
by the author)

non-linear, both materially and culturally determined, and manifest in both
tangible and intangible ways. Migrants bring unique subjective temporalities
to history-making. The aim of this Element is to centre this migrant subjectivity
while accounting for the migrant's institutional and historiographical subjecti-
vation. It consciously reimagines the alternative and even oppositional histories
of post-war migration to Australia, as well as migrant and working-class
orientations to liberal multiculturalism. The Element draws on the Gippsland
Immigration Park as a springboard for such histories and the sociopolitical work
that they can do. I read against the grain or search for silences and gaps in the
tangible and intangible heritage on display.

What does it mean to centre and explore migrant subjectivity, and what perspective does it offer in this Element? It means adopting, at moments, the viewpoint of individual pasts, presents, and futures and the meaning that one makes from this milieu. It also means privileging 'ordinary' storytelling and dispelling empirical or positivist and deterministic understandings of migration history and liberal multiculturalism. In the context of this Element, it also means imagining one (of many) potentially radical subjectivities. The subjective is not universal. In relation to understandings of multiculturalism, it rejects a top-down or institutional approach to the subject matter. Finally, centring migrant subjectivity means turning our critical attention to experience, memory, and emotion as historicised processes. This approach recognises the important role that experience and emotion play in the representation and circulation of collective memories in commemorative contexts.

Adopting the perspective of migrant subjectivity, I argue that migrant (and therefore marginal) heritage processes and constructions have the potential to lay bare the intersectional histories that constitute the collective identity of a place. That is, migrant heritage draws upon memories of displacement, mobility, and settlement that necessarily intersect with changing economic or material conditions. Migrant heritage, approached from the perspective of migrant subjectivity, can also stress the key relationship between labour security and intimate family needs and the historic role of state and institutional structures in shaping daily life. A focus on migrant subjectivity also underlines the central role of emotion and nostalgia in heritage and heritage-making processes. These nostalgic and sometimes ambivalent responses to heritage create possibilities for interpretation that engage with the politics of representation and recognition in multicultural nation states.

The Element, in developing this argument, draws on more than three years of documentary and ethnographic research conducted in Morwell, which has a population of approximately 14,000, and the Latrobe Valley. This included site visits to the Valley and the Park, time spent with local community organisations in their clubhouses and venues, oral history interviews and documentary evidence gathered from the Gippsland Immigration Park Committee and related community groups and local residents, and other primary sources from government bodies investigating heritage, health, environment, and the power industry in the Latrobe Valley. As indicated, my methodology is based on the assumption that knowledge is subjective rather than objective and that an intersectional and sedimented historical approach is required in order to account for how people make meaning from the past.

To offer this local history through a migrant perspective is a productive challenge: it functions as a platform to explore alternative grassroots expressions of multiculturalism from working-class, migrant peoples and to explore their subjective and emotional engagements with wider-circulating historical narratives about the region and the nation's past. The inescapable interconnectedness of labour and migration is a key part of retelling and reimagining this public history. Through this mutual inclusivity (of labour and migration), the migrant subject memories espoused at the Park run counter to those that appear in official documentary records and Authorised Heritage Discourse (AHD) about the region and the nature of its industrial heritage significance.

The Gippsland Immigration Park, as a heritage place, a monument and tribute, a communal meeting point, and an open-air exhibition, is active in the making of local, national, and transnational histories. In reading against the grain or in choosing the settle in the gaps the Park contains, alternative visions of multiculturalisms emerge. The creation and exchange of nostalgic memories of regional community pasts enable transformative possibilities for interpreting the future heritage of this post-industrial place and the role of the migrant subject in it. These alternative readings are worth exploring as examples of the agency of marginalised and marginal voices, highlighting who can or cannot make interventions in well-circulated Australian public histories and official heritage decisions and how they might reveal or conceal past and present inequalities and race-based discriminations.

1 Theoretical and Conceptual Scope

Heritage Studies and Heritage Practice

What I mean by 'heritage' in the context of this Element is shaped by approaches prevalent within the field of critical heritage studies, in which heritage is studied as a 'performative process of meaning making'.[1] As a cultural process and a performance, heritage is not simply a physical fabric, a place, or a thing. To quote Denis Byrne, it 'comes into being' as heritage via both 'the discourse[s] of heritage' and heritage practices and is therefore always intangible.[2] Of course, cultural heritage can be made manifest in the tangible, but it is only made meaningful through the values and stories people attribute to it.[3] Kirshenblatt-Gimblett summarises this well when she states: 'tangible heritage, without intangible heritage, is a mere husk or inert matter'.[4]

---

[1] Laurajane Smith, *Uses of Heritage* (London: Routledge, 2006).

[2] Denis Byrne, 'A Critique of Unfeeling Heritage', in *Intangible Heritage*, ed. Laurajane Smith and Natsuko Akagawa (London: Routledge, 2009), 230.

[3] Dawson Munjeri, 'Tangible and Intangible Heritage: From Difference to Convergence', *Museum International* 56, no. 1–2 (2004): 12–20.

[4] Barbara Kirshenblatt-Gimblett, 'Intangible Heritage as Metacultural Production', *Museum International* 56, no. 1–2 (2004): 60.

As Laurajane Smith asserts, an AHD frames the official designation and categorisation of heritage. Professionals, governments, and their policymakers dominate the AHD: at the global level, it is most readily represented in bodies like UNESCO, their various Conventions concerning conservation and protection of 'the common heritage of humankind', and the World Heritage List. This discourse of heritage works to legitimise and justify particular historical and social narratives, ones that maintain the status quo and render invisible the struggles of marginalised communities. It operates at the national and local level too: a largely fabric-bound, elitist, and Eurocentric AHD prevails in Australia. This heritage discourse is selective in what it celebrates and what it conceals – the intersecting axes of race, gender, and class are not readily accommodated within this discourse, for example. The AHD renders heritage most visible in its monumental and largely Eurocentric form, as a fabric that can only be properly valued and preserved by those with professional expertise and cultural power.[5] Since the 1990s, many scholars have challenged practitioners to re-evaluate heritage management practices and the nature of top-down interventions and have thus challenged the discursive underpinnings of that system. They have consistently called for more involvement and collaboration with local communities and communities of interest and for heritage professionals and policymakers to better integrate community uses and understandings of cultural heritage into conservation practices.[6] The official realm of practice, at the international level, responded with the 2003 UNSECO Convention for Safeguarding of the Intangible Cultural Heritage (ICHC). Australia has yet to ratify this convention. While a move to consider the 'intangible' has had some positive implications for inclusive heritage in Australia – new positions were created for Indigenous traditional owners and consultation became mandatory in many places – there remains the sense that heritage, as a process and discourse, is the reserve of the white-settler cultural majority. Over a decade ago, Waterton and Smith suggested that many heritage projects are done *for* communities rather than *with* them – the result is a consultative, rather than collaborative, approach.[7] Official heritage practices, overseen in Australia by state heritage councils and their agencies, and the use of procedural documents

---

[5] Smith, *Uses of Heritage*.

[6] Starting, in Australia, with Chris Johnston and Australian Heritage Commission, *What Is Social Value? A Discussion Paper* (Canberra: Australian Government Publishing Service, 1992); Emma Waterton, Laurajane Smith, and Gary Campbell, 'The Utility of Discourse Analysis to Heritage Studies: The Burra Charter and Social Inclusion', *International Journal of Heritage Studies* 12, no. 4 (2006): 339–355; Laurajane Smith and Emma Waterton, *Heritage, Communities and Archaeology* (London: Bloomsbury Academic, 2013).

[7] Emma Waterton and Laurajane Smith, 'The Recognition and Misrecognition of Community Heritage', *International Journal of Heritage Studies* 16, no. 1–2 (2010): 4–15.

like Significance Assessments and Conservation Management Plans continue to privilege elitist conceptions of aesthetic value premised on Western ideals that can devalue dynamic and evolving community uses of heritage.

Byrne has critiqued the implications of the ICHC. For Byrne, while the ICHC aspires to be inclusive, UNESCO's 'fantasies of universal value' and the compunction to 'go forth to record and conserve' the intangible means the ICHC does not aid or reflect the type of emotionally laden and socially determined heritage work occurring at the grassroots. However, the ICHC explicitly attempted to avoid replicating the idea of universal value espoused by UNESCO's World Heritage List. The UNESCO-based regime behind the ICHC aimed to facilitate grassroots heritage and community ownership. However, according to Lixinski, they failed in these aims due to weak mechanisms for community participation.[8] Furthermore, state signatories to the ICHC have replicated their understanding of the World Heritage Convention (1972) and ignored or even appropriated minority cultures (and denuded them of the political meaning) when determining what intangible heritage was worthy of international safeguarding. Byrne concludes: 'I believe we would be better employed, first, in examining the politics of visibility in the production of heritage and, second, in reconnecting emotionally to the past via the traces we already have recorded.'[9]

Accordingly, this Element privileges a historical approach to place; the aim is to unpack, from the position of one's subjective experience of the present, migrants' past experiences, behaviours, and relationships in place – and their interstices with present social concerns. This, as Byrne implies, is contrary to much archaeologically compelled heritage work that is more concerned with 'inventorying' potential sites and objects of heritage significance and maintaining the regulated process of so-called expert knowledge.[10] Byrne draws on archaeologist Hamilakis to argue that authorised heritage practice 'denies the potential to engage as feeling beings with past people'.[11] The preoccupation with compiling mass inventories, tied to Western science and ideas of objectivity, hinders empathy and subjectivity or the ability to connect with the *individual humanity* of the past's subjects. I hope this Element offers access to a feeling history, one that does not excise the material past or physical fabric (the remnants of industrial heritage, for example) from their social contexts and the specific circumstances and emotions felt by individual migrant subjects within that space.

---

[8] Lucas Lixinski, 'Selecting Heritage: The Interplay of Art, Politics and Identity', *European Journal of International Law* 22, no. 1 (2011): 81–100.

[9] Byrne, 'A Critique of Unfeeling Heritage', 249.   [10] Ibid., 230.   [11] Ibid., 231.

Since the earliest calls in the 1990s to reassess heritage practice in Australia and realign our approach to 'social value', a body of literature has emerged.[12] These scholars are interested in how to foster community collaboration with the heritage conservation sector and its appointed experts. This has been the case in the Australian literature with regard to Indigenous heritage work over the past two decades. But when it comes to other Others – the ethnicised and therefore non-Anglophone subjects living and working within the settler-colonial state – the research often adopts as case studies institutionally driven or 'co-produced' examples of heritage, rather than examples of practice that emerged from and were controlled by communities themselves.[13] This Element grew out of a concern that too little professional and scholarly attention has been paid to 'subaltern' publics, specifically the (new and older waves of) migrants and ethnic minorities who are the subject of (or sometimes 'add-ons' in) many state-funded exhibitions and commemorations.[14] We need to consider how ethnicised and migrant subjects actively create and publicise their own heritage and history – especially in changing political and social contexts. In settler-colonial countries like Australia and other Anglophone countries like the United Kingdom, the USA, and Canada, the federal government accepted large numbers of permanent settlers in the decades after WWII, but this was also met by recurrent xenophobic opposition. As indicated, further attention needs to be paid to those communities and individuals actively involved in building and publicising their migration and settlement histories and the intersection of these pasts with wider public histories, like post-war labour, industrial development, and deindustrialisation.

Memory Studies and Collective Memory

Debates surrounding the notion of collective memory are extensive. Astrid Erll, in her 2010 *A Companion to Cultural Memory Studies*, opted for the term 'cultural' over collective, partly for the latter's tendency to invoke impassioned

---

[12] Denis Byrne, Helen Brayshaw, and Tracy Ireland, *Social Significance: A Discussion Paper* (Sydney: NSW National Parks and Wildlife Service, 2003); Annie Clarke and Chris Johnston, 'Time, Memory, Place and Land: Social Meaning and Heritage Conservation in Australia', Paper Presented at the Scientific Symposium, ICOMOS 14th General Assembly, Zimbabwe, 2003; Alexandra Dellios, 'Migration Parks and Monuments to Multiculturalism: Finding the Challenge to Australian Heritage Discourses through Community Public History Practice', *The Public Historian* 42, no. 2 (2020): 7–32.

[13] Smith and Waterton, *Heritage, Communities and Archaeology*; Viv Golding and Wayne Modest, eds., *Museums and Communities: Curators, Collections and Collaboration* (London: Bloomsbury, 2013); Barbara Little and Paul Shackel, *Archaeology, Heritage, and Civic Engagement: Working toward the Public Good* (London: Routledge, 2016), 10–25.

[14] Denis Byrne and Maria Nugent, *Mapping Attachment: A Spatial Approach to Aboriginal Post-contact Heritage* (Sydney: Department of Environment and Conservation NSW, 2004).

debate from all disciplines engaging in memory studies. She concludes: 'Cultural [collective] memory hinges on the notion of the medial [material], because it is only via medial externalization (from oral speech to writing, painting or using the Internet) that individual memories, cultural knowledge, and versions of history can be shared.'[15] But where does that leave considerations of the social and psychological in the study of collective memory? Most sociological approaches to memory take their cue from Maurice Halbwachs's seminal works published in the early twentieth century, including *On Collective Memory* and *Social Frameworks of Remembering*. Halbwachs positions memory as a social activity achieved via shared consciousness. He argues that the act of remembering cannot be separated from the social group and the social frameworks that determine memory's articulation. This approach continues to shape the study of memory across disciplines, including history. However, those who adopt a more psychological perspective contest the approach.

Kerwin Lee Klein, taking up criticisms made by psychologists concerned with memory as a cognitive process, stated that 'careful scholars' make 'prefatory disclaimers to ward off charges that they might be indulging in mystical transpositions of individual psychological phenomena onto imaginary collectivities'.[16] This Element has replicated the approach adopted by cultural historians to collective memory: analysing public forms of history – whether monument or museum – as creative material articulations of and responses to collective (or 'cultural') memories. Such an approach does not create imaginary collectives; any analysis of collective memory comments on and responds to subjective constructions of imaginary collectives, for all collectives are essentially imagined, memory being but one mode through which this is achieved.

In this vein, sociologist Alon Confino argues that a more critical approach to memory would consider not only how memory is represented but also how representations are interpreted and received. This reflects larger trends in public history, and more recently in critical heritage studies, that moves us beyond representational analyses or curatorial perspectives.[17] Historian Wulf Kansteiner adopts a similar approach, though he shies away from arguing for Confino's all-encompassing *histoire des mentalités* approach. Rather – and predictably, for a historian – he argues for 'extensive contextualisation' in memory studies and a more considered analysis of the wider social, political,

---

[15] Astrid Erll, 'Cultural Memory Studies: An Introduction', in *A Companion to Cultural Memory Studies*, ed. Ansgar Nunning and Astrid Erll (Berlin: De Gruyter, 2010), 1–2.

[16] Kerwin Lee Klein, 'On the Emergence of Memory in Historical Discourse', *Representations* 69 (2000): 135.

[17] See Laurajane Smith, *Emotional Heritage: Visitor Engagement at Museums and Heritage Sites* (London: Routledge, 2021).

and cultural environment of a memory's construction, reception, and contest-ation. Extensive contextualisation, Kansteiner argues, assists in linking the facts of representation (the tropes on display at the Gippsland Immigration Park, for example) with the facts of reception (their use function, the values they espouse, and their contestation by different publics). This framing is useful for the analysis contained in this Element, but it has its limits too. First, these 'facts' of representation and reception are not self-evident but continuously rearranged by different publics. Keightley and Pickering capture this creative tension in their reflections on the 'active synthesis of remembering and imagination':

> what has been taken over from the past is continually being revised in order to accommodate an open and continually unfolding future ... a commonplace of modernity, with its future-orientated temporality generating a need not only for new experiences but also for the recurrent reassessment of past experiences.[18]

Second, Kansteiner rejects terminology he sees as better suited to discussions about the psychological and emotional dynamics of individual remembering (rather than collective memory). He is not alone here. Kirk Savage argues that unlike psychologists, cultural historians are interested in 'memory in external deposits, located not within people, but within shared public space', which is a fair classification of some work.[19] But extensive contextualisation cannot but incorporate a consideration of the *emotional*, and emotions here are not merely individual cognitive processes and therefore not the reserve of psychological analyses. Emotions are socially mediated, transmitted, and shared; emotions can be politically harnessed and projected for wider social ends.

Studies of emotion in history and heritage have sought to centre the role of certain emotions (love, desire, and attachment; jealousy and anger; pride and dignity) in social movements and as both historically and socially determined phenomena.[20] Exploring the role of emotions has aided the study of collective memory and remembering. For example, scholarship addressing the role of trauma and traumatic events in the memory work of refugees and the forcefully displaced adopts an approach to transnational, transversal, or diasporic memory that is invested in unpacking the relationship between 'memory institutions',

---

[18] Emily Keightley and Michael Pickering, *The Mnemonic Imagination: Remembering as Creative Practice* (London: Palgrave Macmillan, 2012), 7–8.

[19] Kirk Savage cited in Marilyn Lake, ed., *Memory, Monuments and Museums: The Past in the Present* (Melbourne: Melbourne University Press in association with the Australian Academy of the Humanities, 2006), 1.

[20] Laurajane Smith, Margaret Wetherell, and Gary Campbell, *Emotion, Affective Practices and the Past in the Present* (London: Routledge, 2018).

'nationalist imaginaries', and migrant/emigre/refugee/exile subjectivity, which of course includes emotions.[21]

Therefore, Erll's classification of memory studies according to 'material', 'social', or 'mental' approaches is not productive in capturing the trajectory of the field over the past decade, especially in relation to critical heritage studies. This is more than a matter of being interdisciplinary. A consideration of emotions, and new directions in the field of heritage studies that centre community perceptions, also has the result of collapsing the rigid distinction between the individual 'process of remembering and memory as the product resulting from that activity'.[22] Instead, critical heritage studies compel us to consider the inescapably *social* nature of memory and its cross-temporal and multi-scalar constitution. In summary, the nexus between representation and reception, between emotions and social context, will be important in interrogating the political and nostalgic work behind migrant heritage-making in the Latrobe Valley.

Subsequent sections offer multi-layered accounts of the community heritages of the deindustrialising region of the Latrobe Valley. These accounts cannot be undertaken without acknowledging the collective and individual expression of certain emotions associated with these working histories and their retelling, including anger, neglect, pride, and dignity. Sociologists have explored the 'emotional dimensions' of class identities and the politics of class – and these analytical frameworks have become relevant to the study of industrial heritage and the social, cultural, and political, and economic changes within which former industrial structures have been transformed into heritage sites and museums.[23] Within these analytical frameworks – those that consider the emotional and subjective dimensions embedded within heritage performances pertaining to a working-class past – the subject of 'nostalgia' has become especially relevant.

Emotions and Heritage: Nostalgia

Nostalgia, as an emotive charge in collective memory, is central to the analysis offered in subsequent sections. The Gippsland Immigration Park draws on a nostalgic memory of a migrant and working-class past. Nostalgia remains, in much political discourse on the Left, 'reviled as a lie, as the essence of reaction'.[24] As an emotion, it is accused of lacking accuracy and 'taunted as

[21] Marianne Hirsch, 'Stateless Memory', *Critical Times* 2, no. 3 (2019): 419.

[22] Keightley and Pickering, *The Mnemonic Imagination*, 3.

[23] Magdalena Novoa, 'Gendered Nostalgia: Grassroots Heritage Tourism and (De)industrialization in Lota, Chile', *Journal of Heritage Tourism* (2021): 1–19; Christian Wicke, Stefan Berger, and Jana Golombek, eds., *Industrial Heritage and Regional Identities* (London: Routledge, 2018).

[24] Alastair Bonnett, *Left in the Past: Radicalism and the Politics of Nostalgia* (London: Bloomsbury, 2010), 3.

disappointedly subjective'.[25] Alternatively, it has the potential to be progressive and productive by directing the public gaze to the structural impacts of state-led industrial enterprises on intimate, individual, collective, and working-class lives over time.[26] It can be progressive and future-orientated, rather than only reactionary or inherently conservative.

The nostalgic pride associated with the coal mining past is a key narrative of the Latrobe Valley's working-class communities. Journalists and academics looking to examples like Brexit, the rise of Trump, and the (re-)emergence of Hanson's racist One Nation party in Australia note that some deindustrialised working-class communities have lent their support in recent decades to re-emerging populist right-wing parties with anti-immigrant agendas.[27] These readings depict working-class deindustrialised communities as feeling left behind by neoliberal economic policies from the late 1980s and abandoned still by centre-left governments. Populist political campaigns in the West have mobilised emotionally charged narratives about an imagined and racially exclusive past. Other critics and academics, like Ian Watson, Joan Williams, and Nancy Fraser, have cautioned us to not equate the views of right-wing populists with all working-class communities.[28] Watson argued that more qualitative research – including attention to autobiographical storytelling – is required to better understand regional towns and urban fringes, places of high unemployment, and social disadvantage, where new national populism appears to be taking hold. While the Latrobe Valley might fulfil some of these criteria, it hasn't become a stronghold for new national populism. In any case, the motivations and interests of working-class people themselves remain opaque in this debate – despite the breadth of social commentary in the wake of various national elections in Australia, Britain, and America.

The form of nostalgic emotion associated with these working-class identities in deindustrialised communities is often equated with reactionary nationalistic

---

[25] Ibid., 2–3.

[26] Alison Blunt, 'Collective Memory and Productive Nostalgia: Anglo-Indian Home-Making at McCluskieganj', *Environment and Planning D: Society and Space* 21 (2003): 717–738.

[27] Samuel Earle, 'The Toxic Nostalgia of Brexit', *The Atlantic*, 5 October 2017, https://www.theatlantic.com/international/archive/2017/10/brexit-britain-may-johnson-eu/542079/; Justin Gest, *The New Minority: White Working Class Politics in an Age of Immigration and Inequality* (Oxford: Oxford University Press, 2016); David Marr, 'The White Queen: One Nation and the Politics of Race', *Quarterly Essay* 65 (2017): 1–102.

[28] Ian Watson, *A Disappearing World: Case Studies in Class, Gender and Memory* (Melbourne: Scholarly Publishing, 2015); Joan Williams, *White Working Class: Overcoming Class Cluelessness in America* (Boston: Harvard Business Review Press, 2017); Nancy Fraser, 'Progressive Neoliberalism versus Reactionary Populism: A Choice that Feminists Should Refuse', *Nordic Journal of Feminist and Gender Research* 24, no. 4 (2016): 281–284.

politics in Australia. As argued, this nostalgic impetus is complicated in the Valley, a place that benefitted so much from mass immigration and subsequent waves of new arrivals from Asia. Newer and older migrant and ethnicised community groups actively participate in civic life, even in the era of industrial decline. Like other lagging regional centres in Australia, incoming migrants, including people of colour, have been cast as a revitalising force for the local economy in Gippsland.[29] Academics and policy commentators point to the success of various state and federal regional refugee resettlement schemes, especially in Toowoomba in Queensland and Wollongong in New South Wales.[30] However, it is important to also acknowledge that while this 'injection' of new skills from refugee and migrant arrivals is much valued in regional Victoria, the on-the-ground services in the Gippsland region, especially appropriate housing and service providers with adequate cultural knowledge, is still lacking – a situation that is familiar across Australia's entire history of migrant settlement.[31]

Recent studies of the role of nostalgia in heritage making draw on counter-orthodox suggestions that nostalgia can be a source of radical potential. In these suggestions, the sense of 'loss' central to nostalgia is also important to the intersubjective imagination and therefore to reimagining (and temporally projecting) radical politics. These suggestions are counter-orthodox due to historic discourses in the political left – about progress and change – that have cast nostalgia as antithetical to radical and progressive politics. However, Alistair Bonnett in his work on nostalgia unpacks case studies of early English socialism, anti-colonialism, and postcolonialism to argue that nostalgia is an important but rarely acknowledged aspect of the radical imagination. The paradoxical connections between nostalgia and radicalism, he argues, are defined by difficult encounters and repressed allegiances.[32] Other scholars tackling the issue of nostalgia have also argued that as a form of collective memory, nostalgia can renew the historicity of past political struggles, of resistance and organisation, and can therefore form a precondition to new counter-hegemonic struggles.[33] In

---

[29] McDonald, Brooke, Sandy Gifford, Kim Webster, John Wiseman, and Sue Casey. *Refugee Resettlement in Regional and Rural Victoria: Impacts and Policy Issues*. (Melbourne: Victorian Health Promotion Foundation and prepared by the Refugee Health Research Centre, La Trobe University, 2008). https://refugeehealthnetwork.org.au/wp-content/uploads/RefugeeResettlement_Web_Vichealth+report.pdf

[30] www.kaldorcentre.unsw.edu.au/publication/australia%E2%80%99s-post-covid-19-economic-recovery-what%E2%80%99s-role-migrants-and-refugees

[31] https://refugeehealthnetwork.org.au/wp-content/uploads/RefugeeResettlement_Web_Vichealth+report.pdf

[32] Bonnett, *Left in the Past.*

[33] Claire Norton and Mark Donnelly, *Liberating Histories* (London: Routledge, 2018), 109.

heritage studies, these debates have coalesced around analyses of former mining sites, steelworks, railway yards, and factories turned into heritage attractions.[34]

The Park has engendered many points of community and personal exchange and contestation over heritage and history. Nostalgia permeates these exchanges and debates. As Smith and Campbell maintain, considering the key role of emotions like nostalgia in heritage helps us avoid perpetuating 'the myth of professional neutrality defined by the authorised heritage discourse'.[35] Much like the form of nostalgia that Smith and Campbell identified in their study of visitor and staff responses to museums of industrial and working-class heritage, the memories privileged and enabled by the Park are also highly 'imaginative and creative, at times unashamedly maudlin'.[36] Smith and Campbell found across their case studies of industrial heritage in England, the United States, and Australia:

> That which is remembered is done so with a sense of loss tempered with overt pride, empathy and gratitude, which is in turn underlined by a desire to assert a sense of communal belonging and sense of place in the context of rapid deindustrialization and social change. It is also often about valuing the achievements of the past in terms of a set of political and social values that are seen to have underpinned those achievements – habitually a sense of hard work, collective action and progressive politics.

Similarly, as Jarvis and Bonnet found in their urban study, nostalgia can be diverse, ambivalent, and contradictory – residing in attachments to place and time that can be simultaneously negative and positive. Critical engagement with nostalgia, they argue, can expose issues of 'historical persistence' (the use of the past in the present) in all its ambiguity and ambivalence.[37]

Despite identifying elements of a progressive nostalgia expressed at the Park, my reading is also conscious of the power of positivist narratives of state multiculturalism, those narratives contained in revisionist and politically conservative representations of Australia and its harmonious (whitewashed) modern history. The influence of this is seen in the prevalence of the 'migrant success story' in popular representations of the post-war immigration scheme.

---

[34] Stefan Berger and Steven High, '(De-)Industrial Heritage: An Introduction', *Labor* 16, no. 1 (2019): 1–27; Lucy Taksa, Volume 85, 'Machines and Ghosts: Politics, Industrial Heritage and the History of Working Life at the Eveleigh Workshops', *Labour History* (2003): 65–88; Tim Strangleman, 'Mining a Productive Seam? The Coal Industry, Community and Sociology', *Contemporary British History* 32, no. 1 (2018): 18–38.

[35] Laurajane Smith and Gary Campbell, '"Nostalgia for the Future": Memory, Nostalgia and the Politics of Class', *International Journal of Heritage Studies* 23, no. 7 (2017): 615.

[36] Ibid., 613.

[37] Helen Jarvis and Alastair Bonnett, 'Progressive Nostalgia in Novel Living Arrangements: A Counterpoint to Neo-traditional New Urbanism?' *Urban Studies* 50, no. 11 (2013): 2349–2370.

This story tends to erase past, present, and ongoing structural and material inequalities premised on race, racism, and Indigeneity in Australia. These conservative narratives exert an influence over the tropes contained in the Park, but there is more occurring here, as an account of the contested community memories associated with the Park will show. For example, in some cases, these narrative tropes around state multiculturalism operate as a means for the marginal (working-class and longer-resident non-Anglo-Celtic migrant groups) to insert themselves into a mainstream and accepted heritage narrative. The language of state heritage grant applications enables this insertion (or absorption and therefore erasure, depending on your perspective). In this rendering, they are grateful migrants made citizens, who helped build the region during its glorious industrial boom. But we cannot simply cast this as reactionary nostalgia without interrogating further the situational motives and status of such renderings and the subjects implicated in them. That is, the migrant success story/grateful migrant trope can be strategically deployed for other political purposes.

Bella Dicks, in her analysis of class identities and performances at a living history coal-mining museum in South Wales, centred her discussion on emotion. Heritage narratives engage with received ideas about working-class identities, which are also familiar to this study of the Latrobe Valley. Images of defeat, subjection, decline, and neglect are matched by motifs of 'heroic potency', an unstable and vulnerable confluence that reflects the complexity of classed subjectivities in a neoliberal present. Attached to these images and motifs are moral judgements that, Dicks argues, elicit highly emotional responses amongst social actors – 'the emotional reverberations of class are present in heritage, too'.[38]

In this context, the radical potential of nostalgia can be especially potent, for its ability to function as both a collective memory framework and its reliance on an emotional empathy with past subjectivities and classed lives. Understood in these terms, nostalgic counter-hegemonic political work contests 'dominant ways of managing and understanding temporality within the spheres of public life' (state-sanctioned or invented 'traditions' and ceremonies), 'as well as arguing for a preferred narration of a given past' that stresses episodes of collective organisation and struggle.[39] Historians Norton and Donnelly argue activists and political campaigners have made use of the past, of nostalgically charged memories, for counter-hegemonic purposes: 'securing retroactive justice, or placing a contemporary political struggle within a genealogy of

---

[38] Bella Dicks, 'Performing the Hidden Injuries of Class in Coal-Mining Heritage', *Sociology* 42, no. 3 (2008): 440.

[39] Norton and Donnelly, *Liberating Histories*, 109–110.

analogous precedents, activists have often chosen to invoke the past as a store of resources for constructive effect'.[40]

Admittedly, the people behind the Gippsland Immigration Park would not identify themselves as activists. However, for the purposes of this Element, they are approached as 'memory activists'. They make public interventions into historical narratives by centring migrant and working-class histories of organisation and struggle. The collective and contested working-class memories that circulate around migration to the Latrobe Valley are written into (and translated out of) the content, processes, and variegated forms on offer at the Park. They offer a springboard for new, non-linear and dialectical understandings of this past, present, and future. Power dynamics are an important part of this analysis. The authority of the migrant Committee, as well as wider-circulating state-sanctioned narratives about harmonious multiculturalism, is not assumed to be absolute in this alternative reading. The Park as a multi-medium collective memory platform that sought to include many 'new' and 'old' migrant voices and one constructed and received in a contentious local heritage landscape aids many dialogue (and dialogic) exchanges.

The Park also espouses alternative collective memories of migrant mobility and settlement in the region throughout the post-war era, which re/direct the function of nostalgia at the Park to arguably more progressive, reflective, and sometimes future-orientated ends. As subsequent sections will demonstrate, the Park can be read as rejecting superficial ethnic markers as the making of migrant communities, with the result of legitimising migrant-collective political and cultural recognition. These memories stress the hard and dirty work, the impact of family separation, and demonstrate an enduring attachment to the value of communality, organised labour, welfare rights, and job security. The Park's nostalgia even permits a resentment towards the state, industry, and corporations that wrought so much damage to the bodies and social fabric of the Latrobe Valley.

However, this nostalgia is not so amorphous as to be totally inclusive, and all historical narratives contain their partial truths and thus their silences. Women, Australia's First Nations' people (the Gunai Kurnai, the Indigenous group on whose lands the Park was built), children, and adolescents, and undocumented arrivals, are less visible at the Park, though they do make some sideline appearances, as subsequent sections will show.

Contested or Dissonant Heritage

In this reading of the Park, I am consciously searching for challenges to established official and political narratives around multiculturalism, industrialisation,

---

[40] Ibid., 110.

and deindustrialisation. Those contested heritages can be summarised through a few contradictory or binary collective memories: the nostalgic memories around the bountiful and steady labour provided by the Valley's coal mining and power stations, matched by memories of poor workplace health and safety, long-term health effects, and the fall-out from privatisation and feelings of abandonment and anger towards the state government; the celebrated influx of much-needed post-war migrant labour matched by recollections of loneliness and continued mobility across Australia, workplace discrimination and poor housing for non-English-speaking migrants; and of course, the contradictory public emotions expressed about the sight, smell, and sounds of industry and their immediate and long-term environmental impacts, and whether to commemorate, conceal, or destroy the mammoth remnants of this industry in the landscape of the Latrobe Valley.

These heritages are contested but not 'dissonant', dissonance being an approach that can effectively cast heritage as a 'series of individualisms'.[41] In their book *The Politics of Heritage: The Legacies of Race,* Littler and Naidoo explore a model of heritage that is 'a more open process, one which shows how various inheritances interconnect, and can be changed through encounters, rather than the constantly individualised model of elevating someone's heritage at the expense of someone else's'.[42] That approach is also reflected in the public history practices of the University of Hertfordshire Heritage Hub historians Sarah Lloyd and Julie Moore. They coin the term 'sedimented histories' to summarise their approach to creating collaborative and co-produced regional histories in England:

> Where voices and memories are contested or perspectives fragmented, where elements of the past are differently weighted or valued, we are aiming to create a 'sediment' of connected, but not necessarily uniform histories: rather like Raphael Samuel's view of the built environment as 'a sediment of geological strata, a multi-layered reality', sedimented histories are available over time, adjacent to one another, but not thrust into a competition for survival of the historically fittest.[43]

This approach to the practice of public history, and its analysis, shapes the alternative readings consciously sought in this work's analysis of the Park. What happens when we allow 'histories to settle alongside one another'? Lloyd and Moore suggest that it may encourage us to 'recognise the differences and

---

[41] Jo Littler and Roshi Naidoo, eds., *The Politics of Heritage: The Legacies of Race* (London: Routledge, 2004), 7.

[42] Ibid.

[43] Sarah Lloyd and Julie Moore, 'Sedimented Histories: Connections, Collaborations and Co-production in Regional History', *History Workshop Journal* 80, no. 1 (2015): 242.

connections between them, to experiment with context and scale, and to acknowledge, if not always adopt, the rituals and associations loaded onto them'.[44]

This can be a consciously oppositional analysis in some cases: within the extant historiography and in public history narratives of the Valley, migrant, industrial, and labour heritages do not often appear as intertwined, let alone sedimented.[45] The long history of race and ethnicity in the region, in particular, is not readily drawn upon as a resource in the promotion of the Latrobe Valley's heritage, even as it extends to the 'pioneering' era of Gippsland's history. As subsequent sections will unpack, with the exception of the Park, the frames of remembrance that dominate the region's (and specifically Morwell town's) public history – the memorials and memorial gardens, heritage walks, council-funded local histories, historical societies, and their small museums – do not consider the migrant or even non-Anglo-Australian perspective, or the relationship between migration and industrial labour.

Historian Erik Eklund from the Centre for Gippsland Studies has explored the 'agents of influence' that have promoted the region's heritage: at an official and governmental level, he argues that industrial heritage has yet to be recognised as an economic and cultural resource; at the vernacular and informal level, there are some examples of a desire to commemorate the recent industrial and coal-mining past, despite and perhaps because of the trauma of privatisation and widespread job losses.[46] In addition, the reality of climate change has only recently become a part of local rhetoric and begun to complicate these local public heritage narratives, although the more immediate environmental and health impacts of the coal industry has been felt and debated by some residents of the Valley since the 1920s, as subsequent sections will demonstrate. There is little mention of the migrant heritage of the region, let alone non-Anglophone heritage *as part of* other heritages.

Heritage and Recognition, Heritage and Subjectivity

When people reconstruct and negotiate the past, they partake in performative acts of remembering – that can draw on shared and externalised resources – which in

---

[44] Ibid., 244.

[45] The latter concerned with the people; the former with the 'technologies, with sites of work and workforce development'. See Keir Reeves, Erik Eklund, Andrew Reeves, Bruce Scates, and Vicki Peel, 'Broken Hill: Rethinking the International Significance of the Material Culture and Intangible Heritage of the Australian Labour Movement', *International Journal of Heritage Studies* 17, no. 4 (2011): 301–317.

[46] Erik Eklund, '"There Needs to be Something There for People to Remember": Industrial Heritage in Newcastle and the Hunter Valley, Australia', in *Industrial Heritage and Regional Identities*, ed. Christian Wicke, Stefan Berger, and Jana Golombek (London: Routledge, 2018), 157.

turn inform their present and future imaginings. In this process, people draw on a range of emotions to affirm and remake personal and collective narratives. These heritage processes and performances are also, as Smith asserts, intimately implicated in the politics of recognition: of asserting, negotiating, or legitimising claims for recognition (within and from the body politic).[47] The affording or withholding of cultural recognition ('being rendered invisible via the authoritative representational, communicative, and interpretative practices of one's culture') is an inescapably intersubjective process.[48]

In his analysis, Gnecco frames 'multicultural heritage' as a commodity and a device regulated by state and multilateral agencies. This multiculturalism, he argues, masks the lived inequalities of populations in favour of a 'phantasmatic diversity'. He refers to the *limits of recognition* for minority groups and the constraints on their ability to command space in public forums and challenge prevailing power structures:

> [T]he multicultural conviviality of cultural diversity has not meant recognizing the worth of the different but merely its existence, which has thus been organized and, to a large extent, isolated. . . . Real and lived inequalities have been masked by a phantasmatic diversity. The result is perversely violent: unbearable inequalities appear as desirable diversities.[49]

The modern politics of multiculturalism in Australia can be categorised accordingly. But this ahistorical framing also perpetuates silences; it masks decades of 'migrant rights activism', for one. This migrant-led movement was subsumed by a state-sanctioned multicultural rhetoric from the 1980s. Migrant rights activists demanded from mainstream institutions and government better political representation and participation for ethnic minority groups – a 'parity of participation' that has arguably never been achieved in a multicultural Australia. These demands were premised on material conditions that constrained the migrant subject's ability to live and work, especially if they had English as a second or additional language. Underlying these material demands was a politics of recognition, an argument for the retention and public and political acceptance of their cultural heritages, a matter they saw as indivisible from the distribution of material resources. Philosopher Nancy Fraser articulated this idea in the wake of neoliberal reform, arguing that no redistribution or recognition can occur without representation:

---

47 Smith, *Emotional Heritage.*

48 Nancy Fraser, 'From Redistribution to Recognition? Dilemmas of Justice in a "Post-Socialist" Age', *New Left Review* I/211 (July 1995).

49 Christobal Gnecco, 'Heritage in Multicultural Times', in *The Palgrave Handbook of Contemporary Heritage Research*, ed. Emma Waterton and Steve Watson (London: Palgrave Macmillan, 2015), 266.

> Instead of simply endorsing or rejecting all of identity politics *simpliciter*, we should see ourselves as presented with a new intellectual and practical task: that of developing a *critical* theory of recognition, one which identifies and defends only those versions of the cultural politics of difference that can be coherently combined with the social politics of equality. In formulating this project, I assume that justice today requires *both* redistribution *and* recognition.[50]

How does this relate to our discussion of collective memory, working-class nostalgia, and migrant heritage in the Latrobe Valley? Struggles over collective memory are struggles over identity; studies of heritage and museums have long accepted that public disputes over cultural heritage are about the collective assertion of identity. They are mired in the injustices of recognition and misrecognition, over whose history and culture will be recognised and how. Fraser's work attempted to conceptualise both cultural recognition and social equality 'in ways that support rather than undermine one another', which meant theorising how 'economic disadvantage and cultural disrespect are currently entwined with and support one another'.[51] She recognises too that in practice, economic injustice and cultural injustice are intertwined, 'interimbricated so as to reinforce one another dialectically'.[52]

Laurajane Smith conducted extensive surveys in her work on the embodied performative practices of meaning making that visitors to immigration museums undertake. Heritage was a resource of power, drawn on to validate claims for the recognition of (racial) diversity; conversely, the *mis*recognition of heritage was deployed to maintain the political marginalisation of diversity.[53] As Smith asserts, these identity claims draw on historical and contemporary acknowledgements (or denials) of inequity. That is, they ultimately serve to also make claims over the distribution of material resources. The point here is that heritage is intimately connected to political debates and social justice issues and can have material implications. Yaniv Pora et al., in their survey work, also imply that heritage as an emotional resource can compel political action and the offer of recognition (and again, this implicates the radical potential of nostalgic memory work).[54] In the context of state multiculturalism, where the allocation of funding to the 'right' ethnic groups is premised on their public visibility and acceptance, this politics of recognition is vital to cultural and social survival.

However, as Gnecco has already hinted, a politics of recognition as it has been deployed in the immigration studies literature is not without issue. An

---

[50] Fraser, 'From Redistribution to Recognition?'.   [51] Ibid.   [52] Ibid.

[53] Laurajane Smith, '"We are ... We are Everything": The Politics of Recognition and Misrecognition at Immigration Museums', *Museum and Society* 15, no. 1 (2017): 69–86.

[54] Yaniv Poria, Richard Butler, and David Airey, 'The Core of Heritage Tourism', *Annals of Tourism Research* 30, no. 1 (2003): 238–254.

approach that looks to subjectivities in a white-settler space – whether that be Australian popular culture or elite cultural institutions – cannot be 'radical' if it does not also refuse the discursive and systemic erasure of Indigenous voices and lives. Furthermore, if migrant subjectivity does not extend its sense of contingency, its empathic and intersubjective approach to historical 'what ifs' (based on the affects and effects of displacement), then it becomes a part of the rhetorical violence of Anglo-Saxon supremacy. The latter is premised on the existence of legal categories and a national subjecthood that derives its power from colonial legacies. This underlies many critiques of a politics of recognition, which compels us to consider the Indigenous response to a colonial politics of recognition.[55] Drawing on this tradition, legal scholar Nadine El-Enany rejects a politics of recognition in her scholarship on race, law, and the legacies of empire in Britain today. El-Enany argues that 'colonial dispossession not only determined the contemporary distribution of material wealth, but also radically altered subjectivity in the Fanonian sense of what people desire, consider themselves to as entitled to and understand themselves to be'.[56] To then laud a politics of recognition in this context – in which Othered people are 'permitted' to access to wealth and resources accumulated by the settler-colonial state – is a bankrupt form of migrant solidarity today, and a less-than-radical deployment of nostalgia. This 'statist politics of recognition' involves the 'inclusion' of the racialised (or ethnicised) in the colonial state, but does little to challenge the hostile environment towards so-called illegal people that we witness today. It also does little to de-centre Anglophone entitlement. Drawing on Fanon, she talks instead of a reconceptualisation of regularised migration as anti-colonial resistance, a counter-pedagogy to that of current immigration law (and its legacies).[57] El-Enany proposes a subjectivity different to that in recognition-based arguments. Specifically, she calls for racialised people policed by the colonial state to reimagine themselves as being collectively entitled to the reclamation of wealth accumulated via colonial dispossession. This approach rejects established legal categories and ways of discussing settlement. It embraces a redistribution and radical politics of racial justice, extending on the limits of Fraser's 'no redistribution or recognition without representation'.

Such arguments helped me to realign my somewhat misguided embrace of a politics of recognition, rooted as it was in my inheritance of a post-war

---

[55] Glen Sean Coulthard, *Red Skin White Masks: Rejecting the Colonial Politics of Recognition* (Minneapolis: University of Minnesota Press, 2014).

[56] Nadine El-Enany, *(B)ordering Britain: Law, Race and Empire* (Manchester: Manchester University Press, 2020), 28.

[57] Ibid., 35.

Southern European migrant and working-class politics. It still stands that the migrant subjectivities at the heart of the Gippsland Immigration Park speak within a narrower, Eurocentric politics of recognition, and the limits of this frame of reference are explored in subsequent sections. The Park's political work seeks a form of redistributive justice limited by the confines of the welfare state, and therefore stops short of the radical reimagining of racial subjectivity (and its relationship to and demands on the colonial state) that El-Enany proposes. That is to say, the Park's historicity and recognition-based political work has little to offer by way of empowering Indigenous subjects or other racialised peoples historically subjugated by the settler-colonial state. Its radical potential is stymied here, but not eradicated. It must also be stated that an assimilationist approach is not inherent in all articulations of a politics of recognition. In this ambiguous and at-times contradictory commemorative space, many things are happening that undo the certainty of narratives around Australian nationhood, progress, and industry, and of celebratory state multiculturalism.

Given these limitations, why continue to draw on a politics of recognition when studying heritage? Smith articulates this best when she explains:

> [T]he politics of recognition is indivisible from heritage. This is because whenever the idea that heritage constitutes identity is invoked, heritage immediately becomes implicated in struggles over recognition. These struggles may equally include the maintenance of dominant or received identities and the social and historical narratives that underpin them, as much as they also challenge those identities and narratives and the instances of misrecognition they may maintain.[58]

In state efforts to extend recognition to those rendered ethnically Other in Australia (non-Anglophone), recognition is bound by the superficial limits of 'ethnic contributions' to a 'white managerial multicultural nation-state'.[59] As indicated, the politics of recognition, as a conceptual framework and political philosophy, could be conceptualised as a means to reassess the past and advocate for a 'parity of participation' in Australian society.

Like working-class nostalgia, a politics of recognition has potential to focus attention on the historical and contemporary injustices of material distribution. Clearly, the limits of a recognition-based approach lie in its assimilationist undertones: in the context of settler-colonial Australia, it can demonstrate a disinclination to empower racialised people and to radically reimagine and

---

[58] Smith, *Emotional Heritage*, 49.

[59] Ghassan Hage, *White Nation: Fantasies of White Supremacy in a Multicultural Society* (London: Routledge, 2012).

replace those existing systems premised on centuries of colonial exploitation. A token gesture towards representation – a 'rainbow community' on Australian morning television, for example – does little to challenge our politics and compel structural change. The national public debate continues, especially around Australia's protection of statues and monuments to colonisers, in contrast to the wanton destruction of Indigenous sacred sites. Monuments are mostly markers of colonial, racial, and class violence, which was exported across the Anglophone world through empire building from the nineteenth century. They are powerful symbols of the erasure of non-Anglophone lives, before and during the ongoing process of colonisation.

In 2020, the Australian government planned to mark the 250th anniversary of Captain Cook's voyage along the east coast of Australia by committing millions of dollars to commemorative projects, including the erection of more statues of Cook.[60] In that same year, mining giant Rio Tinto blasted away Aboriginal rock shelters in the Pilbara, which were sacred to the Puutu Kunti Kurrama traditional landowners. Weeks later, as Black Lives Matter protests were staged across the country, and newspapers like *The Guardian* called for the removal of statues that perpetuate the colonial myth of *terra nullius*, NSW law enforcement were deployed to protect the statue of Capitan Cook in Sydney's Hyde Park from vandals.[61] This statue, erected in 1879, still bears the inscription: 'Discovered this territory 1770.' Its protection demonstrated a double standard that 'laid bare Australia's bizarre aggrandisement of whiteness – and the infrastructure that reinforces it'.[62] As Patrick Mercer summarised in his commentary, monuments are about power dynamics; they reflect the stories we are willing to accommodate, and difference is not accommodated.

The sites inscribed on the Australian National Heritage List as 'significant' perpetuate and prop up an unequal system of power relations that work to legitimise and normalise inequity. Occasional inclusions of ever-more 'diverse' places to this list has only come about through concerted decades-long advocacy, or one-off state-funded projects to 'educate' respective ethnic minorities about how they might be included in Australia's heritage.[63] Perhaps this is not the best way to challenge the overall logic of the list, or to challenge the

---

[60] www.arts.gov.au/what-we-do/cultural-heritage/250th-anniversary-captain-cooks-voyage-australia

[61] www.smh.com.au/national/why-the-statues-must-fall-20200612-p5521s.html

[62] Patrick Mercer, 'Australia's Double Standard on Statues and Sacred Sites', *Kill Your Darlings*, 30 August 2020, www.killyourdarlings.com.au/article/australias-double-standard-on-statues-and-sacred-sites/

[63] Most exemplified through Australian Heritage Commission's Migrant Heritage Kit: Australian Heritage Commission and Helen Armstrong, *Migrant Heritage Places in Australia: A Guide – How to Find Your Heritage Places* (Canberra: Commonwealth of Australia, 1995).

Eurocentric underpinnings of heritage management practice and the national narratives behind them. But in some respects, representation and a politics of recognition can generate difficult questions for society about the effects of ongoing injustices, and can be a useful way to approach some minority perspectives and emotions towards the concept of heritage. Representation for these groups matters; it is deeply felt and it has political implications. In some of its more radical deployments, a politics of recognition can extend our vision beyond the limits of state-sanctioned multiculturalism as it is framed in neoliberal nation states.

Multiculturalism, Race, and Heritage

Conventional histories of multiculturalism privilege a top-down perspective, much like the AHD.[64] In public discussions, politicians and journalists discuss multiculturalism as 'a set of policies concerned with management and containment of diversity by nation states'.[65] Multiculturalism, as a loosely conceived set of policies and as a celebratory rhetoric, is also about progress. It maintains a linear view of history: migrants 'become' Australians, and in turn contribute to the nation state. In its focus on progress, it masks past and ongoing inequalities. It stresses consumer choice and consumption. The neoliberal logic of multiculturalism, as it has developed in Western nation states since the 1970s, transforms 'difference' into a symbolic performance by 'ethnics', which becomes visible as a market-driven commodity rather than something with social needs and requiring social care. In effect, this neoliberal agenda has devolved state services to consultancy bodies working for ethnic minority groups while maintaining a loose rhetoric of minority rights within the limits of citizenship. Like its iterations in the United Kingdom and Canada, Australian multiculturalism lauds the successful integration of Others into a harmonious whole, which is nonetheless still dominated by representations of homogeneous whiteness.[66] The case study of Gippsland Immigration Park provides a means to locate a grassroots and migrant-initiated challenge to the limits of these historical narratives.

---

[64] Mark Lopez, *The Origins of Multiculturalism in Australian Politics, 1945–1975* (Melbourne: Melbourne University Press, 2000); Eric Richards, *Destination Australia: Migration to Australia since 1901* (Sydney: University of New South Wales Press, 2008); Gwenda Tavan, *The Long Slow Death of White Australia* (Carlton North: Scribe, 2005); John Hirst, *Sense and Nonsense in Australian History* (Melbourne: Black Inc., 2009).

[65] Amanda Wise and Selvaraj Velayutham, 'Introduction: Multiculturalism and Everyday Life', in *Everyday Multiculturalism*, ed. Amanda Wise and Selvaraj Velayutham (London: Palgrave Macmillan, 2009), 15.

[66] Similar critiques of multiculturalism in the United Kingdom offered by Sneja Gunew, *Haunted Nations: The Colonial Dimensions of Multiculturalisms* (London: Routledge, 2013); Littler and Naidoo, *The Politics of Heritage*.

Political scientists and anthropologists in the United Kingdom, Canada, and Australia have criticised multiculturalism's tendency to essentialise cultural identities, and its failure to account for the cosmopolitan and relational way in which we form our identities.[67] The earliest of these criticisms could also be tied to important work in radical anti-racism that emerged in Britain from the 1970s, especially around the work of Stuart Hall and his contemporaries. Hall and others, including Catherine Hall and Paul Gilroy, explored the interconnectedness of global race relations, underpinned by colonial exploitation, and the boundaries of modernist nation states in perpetuating racialised exploitation.[68] Bonnet argues that these radical anti-racist works, by centring race as a modality through which anti-capitalist conflict was to be fought, rejected the old 'white left', a declining force from the 1980s; this too is a reason why the nostalgia expressed by and for this old white left has been cast by some contemporaries as reactionary and xenophobic.[69]

These works took more time to influence Australian historical scholarship, where many earlier labour histories, and popular Leftist discourses, declined to consider race and ethnicity as a necessary medium through which to understand class relations in Australian society.[70] However, some non-Anglo-Australian political scientists and political philosophers since the 1970s have adopted approaches in Hall's cultural studies school of thought. Jakubowicz, Nicolacopoulos and Vassilacopoulos, and Kakakios and Van Der Velden from the 1970s onwards critiqued the political function of liberal multiculturalism in Australia, and what it did to earlier socialist framings of migrant and working-class solidarity. Philosophers Toula Nicolacopoulos and George Vassilacopoulos, in their study of 'migrant rights activists' within Melbourne's Greek-speaking workers leagues of the 1950s and 1960s, thus produced the following historical narrative about the emergence of multiculturalism from the 1970s:

> Within the revised Anglophone discursive framework [of multiculturalism] organised community life can become focused on the cultivation and enjoyment of ethnic difference to such an extent that the political question of the promotion of democratic community processes has become an incidental concern ... the gradual removal of the question of the fundamental nature

---

[67] Tariq Modood, *Multiculturalism* (Cambridge: Polity Press, 2013).

[68] Stuart Hall, *Fateful Triangle: Race, Ethnicity, Nation*, ed. Kobena Mercer (Cambridge, MA: Harvard University Press, 2017); Paul Gilroy, *There Ain't No Black in the Union Jack: The Cultural Politics of Race and Nation* (London: Hutchinson, 1987); Catherine Hall, 'Doing Reparatory History: Bringing "Race" and Slavery Home', *Race & Class* 60, no. 1 (2018): 3–21.

[69] Bonnet, *Left in the Past*, 122.

[70] Marilyn Lake and Henry Reynolds, *Drawing the Global Colour Line: White Men's Countries and the Question of Racial Equality* (Melbourne: Melbourne University Publishing, 2008). For earlier alternative approaches to labour and class history, see Gill Bottomley and Marie M. de Lepervanche, eds., *Ethnicity, Class, and Gender in Australia* (Sydney: Allen & Unwin, 1984).

of democratic citizenship from the political landscape of the ethnic communities in the post-multiculturalism era.[71]

The matter of how to approach race and ethnicity – and the processes by which people are ethnicised and racialised – in modern Australia is routinely debated. Literary scholar Sneja Gunew explored the utility of ethnicity and race today, and ultimately questioned whether ethnicity, as a category, took over from race:

> because there was a retreat from the 'scientific racism' of an earlier era, or does it in fact represent a new racism (as argued by Balibar and others) where the focus on culture (designated culturalism) serves to camouflage issues to do with unequal power relations?[72]

However, debates essentially circle around the same problems: what structural and systemic issues are at stake in the language of race and ethnicity, and whose interests are being served by the prevailing rhetoric around multiculturalism? This too is a question about the public recognition afforded to migrant and marginalised peoples, and as Gnecco argues in relation to 'multicultural heritage as a global commodity', multiculturalism has had the effect of denuding the 'political voice' of migrant peoples.

Moves away from multiculturalism in countries like the United Kingdom and Germany, where it has been proclaimed a 'failure', are not a departure but rather a continuation of multiculturalism's aims. Concepts like integration and social inclusion – and indeed, more assmilationist framings of 'recognition' – are part of the 'double-edged' sword of corporatised multiculturalism.[73] Again, the issues at stake are structural and systemic, as Littler and Naidoo explain in relation to the United Kingdom: Black and Asian people may be 'pulled into' some mainstream representations, or afforded some visibility,

> but these images don't necessarily reflect available establishment structures or life opportunities. It's an easy celebration of multiculturalism that shores up its celebration by ignoring unequal power relations of the past . . . skates over contemporary inequalities and roots in racialized, gendered, economic exploitations within our heritage.[74]

---

[71] Toula Nicolacopoulos and George Vassilacopoulos, 'On the Methodology of Greek-Australian Historiography', in *Greek Research in Australia: Proceedings of the Biennial International Conference of Greek Studies*, ed. Elizabeth Close, Michael Tsianikas, and George Frazis (Adelaide: Flinders University, 2005), 283.

[72] Gunew, *Haunted Nations*, 20.

[73] Jo Littler and Roshi Naidoo, 'White Past, Multicultural Present: Heritage and National Stories', in *Cultural Heritage: Critical Concepts in Media and Cultural Studies*, Volume 11, ed. Laurajane Smith (Oxon: Routledge, 2006), 108.

[74] Ibid., 108–109.

More radical formations would link the inequalities of the past with the inequalities of the present. In the literature, this is also a matter of reconnecting radical race studies with migration studies, and with labour histories – intersectional and temporal accounts that can leave room for sedimented histories and the lived experiences of ethnicised and racialised peoples.

Multiculturalism and Indigenous Australia

Years after the Gippsland Immigration Park was launched in 2007, the Committee included a new heritage trail that fringes the Park, and extends beyond it to circle around Kernot Lake. It recognises the region's prior Indigenous heritage, and the wider histories that shaped migration and migrants in Gippsland. It is a history of Gippsland's 'development', and therefore privileges industrial progress and the role of coal (like much of the original Gippsland Immigration Park). Its seventy-two panels on the history of Gippsland begins with the Gunai Kurnai nation as the traditional owners of the land. Like the 2007 Opening of the Wall of Recognition, the Committee describes the 'Kurnai' as the original inhabitants of Gippsland, resident in the region for '20,000' years. The Park's Souvenir booklet from 2007 mentions that Indigenous peoples numbered 4,000 when the first Europeans 'entered' Gippsland in the 1840s; they go on to mention the Highland Scots explorers, but not the dispossession and the destruction of Indigenous lands and cultural life that they wrought.[75]

Even grassroots and professedly left-wing community discourses about multiculturalism deal uncomfortably with the relationship between ethnic minority belonging and Indigenous sovereignty. Many established organisations and groups, including the Ethnic Communities Council of Victoria, have recognised that their claims to national belonging cannot be made without first acknowledging the separate status and unceded sovereignty of First Nation's peoples. Some (not all) see alliances over social justice demands as the only way forward to a reconciled Australia.[76] In the 1960s, migrant rights activists on the far left drew on a language of working-class solidarity and took some of their cues from the Indigenous civil rights movement. But the issue of language and common goals remains a point of debate between groups. As Yugambeh (Munanjali) and South Sea Islander academic Chelsea Bond stated, 'a reconciliation that speaks of diversity but not sovereignty as unceded is dispossessing'.[77]

---

[75] Gippsland Immigration Park Committee, 'Gippsland Immigration Wall of Recognition: Souvenir Booklet – Official Opening, March 18th 2007', 2007.

[76] George Zangalis, 'Time for Our Voices to be Heard-Representation by Election Not Selection', Public Statement, 2019.

[77] Chelsea Bond Twitter, @drcbond. See also Chelsea Bond, 'We Just Black Matter: Australia's Indifference to Aboriginal Lives and Land', *The Conversation*, 16 October 2017, https://thecon

The 'continuously disturbed underpinning' in celebrations of multiculturalism offered by Australian politicians is the unresolved relationship between descendants of immigrants and Indigenous nations.[78] Some migrant and ethnic community celebrations and their rhetoric are complicit in dispossession, and the rhetoric of the Australian nation state, through the discourse of multiculturalism, supports and propels this dispossession. Multiculturalism was and is premised on celebratory nationalism. It builds on and perpetuates the silences around histories of race, racism, and Indigeneity. It is therefore imperative that we also explore the prior and continuing Indigenous heritage associated with the lands on which the Gippsland Immigration Park rests, as a matter of fully extending the politics of recognition (beyond diverse and ethnicised migrant groups) and countering the dispossessing impetus of state multiculturalism.

The Gunai Kurnai nation, on whose lands the Park resides, is made up of five clans with diverse cultural heritages and language groups: the Brabralung (people of Central Gippsland), Brataualung (South Gippsland), Brayakaulung (around the current town of Sale), Krauatungalung (near the Snowy River), and Tatungalung (near Lakes Entrance on the coast).[79] I found no evidence that the Gippsland Immigration Park Committee consulted with local Indigenous groups in forming these panels.

For visitors wanting more, there is the adjacent Aboriginal Waterhole Creek Cultural Heritage Trail, a project initiated and created in 2015 by Park Tracks and Latrobe City Council, featuring the artistic murals of Gunai Kurnai man Ronald Edwards. Park Tracks and the Council also sought partnership with the Gunai Kurnai Land and Water Aboriginal Corporation (GLAWAC) and the Ramahyuck Aboriginal District Corporation, alongside other government bodies, but the management remains the preserve of local government. Edwards' bright and alluring murals are storytelling about the land, a means to break down barriers, and build understanding about the different storytelling, tribal markings, men and women's designs, and multiple language groups of the Gunai Kurnai. The first panel reads *Gnokan Danna Murra Kor-ki* ('give me your hand my friend'). As Ronald Edwards explains in the second of the nine panels that mark the walk:

---

versation.com/we-just-black-matter-australias-indifference-to-aboriginal-lives-and-land -85168; Chelsea Bond, 'The Audacity of Anger', *IndigenousX*, 29 January 2018, https://indi genousx.com.au/chelsea-bond-the-audacity-of-anger/.

[78] Andrew Jakubowicz, 'The Realities of Australian Multiculturalism', in *'For Those Who've Come Across the Seas': Australian Multicultural Theory, Policy and Practice*, ed. Andrew Jakubowicz and Christina Ho (Melbourne:Australian Scholarly Publishing, 2013), 3.

[79] Gunaikurnai Land and Waters Aboriginal Corporation (GLaWAC) 2021, https://gunaikurnai .org.au/about-glawac/

Figure 2 'The Welcome Mural', panel one of Aboriginal Waterhole Creek
Cultural Heritage Trail (sourced from: https://walkingmaps.com.au/walk/3076;
permission granted from Victoria Walks)

> My traditional art designs carry my identity, identifies my country, along with
> the stories and meanings to my cultural heritage. . . . This art work is about
> Aboriginal Gunai Kurnai Country and the story telling of the land. As you can
> see in this artwork, it is about a person who helps out within our community
> and the wider general community to help break down barriers in today's
> world. I want people to understand and know that Aboriginal people have
> different markings, designs, stories and different language groups which
> cover South Eastern Gippsland. . . . We want to share our knowledge with
> the non-Indigenous community.[80]

Edwards goes on to explain that the dot paintings that dominate popular depictions of Indigenous art are uncommon in the southern regions; they are more
prominent in northern parts of Australia. The circles and triangles utilised in the
Gunai Kurnai designs, and which change according to men's and women's
designs, represent different tribes of the Gunai Kurnai nation. Another panel
displays the five clans of the Gunai Kurnai and their shields, each with
a distinctive design. In the design of this walk, the communities are determined
to express the way Gunai Kurnai culture is distinct and varied, and they do so
through language and visual representations.

---

[80] Ronald Edwards, Sign 2, on the Aboriginal Waterhole Creek Cultural Trail Walk 2015, https://
walkingmaps.com.au/walk/3076

Edwards and GLAWAC's contributions were central to the Heritage Trail, and the consultative approach adopted by Park Tracks. Involving traditional owners in the management of country, in the preservation of language, associations, and environmental conservation efforts, has been recognised as central to 'best' heritage practice.[81] But these consultative practices – and the truth telling they enable – still struggle to deal with legacies of colonialism, and the stories (and structures) imposed on the Gunai Kurnai peoples and their lands since the advent of European colonisation. These are layered histories of place that have been historically erased or avoided.

The main intention of the Aboriginal Waterhole Creek Cultural Heritage Trail in Morwell is to showcase the area's natural beauty, and the land's intimate ties to Indigenous culture. For example, it showcases the role of native Black Wattle in creating boomerangs, or the use of Kangaroo Apple as a contraceptive. To what extent, however, does it account for post-contact landscapes and potential impacts of colonialism on attachments to (and therefore changing uses of) particular locales? Maria Nugent noted that Australian heritage registers tend to confine Aboriginal culture to the pre-contact era, listing sites and artefacts that point to an 'authentic' traditional Indigenous society, while rarely noting the significance of other buildings and places to Aboriginal people since 1788.[82] This AHD can present a 'false picture of Aboriginality', which ignores evolving attachments to local places, whether that be an altered but continued relationship to country or one that is severed due to the experience of forced dispersal, child removal, and segregation by state authorities and religious organisations.[83]

The trail is not a memorial space that explicitly engages with the past and present politics of relations between Indigenous and non-Indigenous peoples, or the unresolved histories of displacement that rest at the heart of more recent 'history wars' specific to the region. The question then becomes: Do all heritage sites marking and sharing local Indigenous cultures need to engage with stories of dispossession, and potentially victimhood? Is there a risk that collectively these monuments create a pervasive notion of victimhood for Indigenous people whose historical occupation is being acknowledged?

In this space, white-settler heritage practitioners need to be weary of the 'paralysis of integrity': the feeling of discomfort by non-Indigenous peoples over 'fear that you might cause offence or make a mistake', which can sometimes

---

[81] Maria Nugent, 'Mapping Memories: Oral History for Aboriginal Cultural Heritage in New South Wales, Australia', in *Oral History and Public Memories*, ed. Paula Hamilton and Linda Shopes (Philadelphia: Temple University Press, 2008), 47–63. See also Byrne and Nugent, *Mapping Attachment*.

[82] Nugent, 'Mapping Memories', 48.

[83] Ibid. See also Heather Goodall, *Invasion to Embassy: Land in Aboriginal Politics in New South Wales, 1770–1972* (Sydney: Sydney University Press, 2008).

function as a justification for ignorance, wilful silence, or stasis.[84] Guidelines like the Australian Heritage Commission's 2002 'Ask First: A guide to respecting Indigenous heritage places and values' (though in need of proper enforcements and state incentives) function as a starting point for heritage practitioners.[85] One of the stated aspirations of GLAWAC is to work productively alongside Parks Victoria staff, and other government bodies, in the management of country and in the sharing of cultural knowledge.[86] This forms part of their stated 'right to use, manage and control our resources', which evokes principles from the United Nations Declaration on the Rights of Indigenous Peoples.[87] Through the practice of co-management, and in its presentation, the Waterhole Creek Cultural Heritage Trail has the potential to begin important conversations – ones that have the effect of extending belonging and understanding to non-Indigenous visitors to the country. In this way, this heritage site, like other efforts across the country, is not mired in victimhood, but is active in the sovereignty struggle.

However, in relation to the political geography of Morwell and the untold stories that frame this Cultural Heritage Trail and the adjacent Gippsland Immigration Park, certain silences are deafening. For example, in 2020, Black Lives Matter protests reignited similar debates about structural racism in Australia, and the Gippsland hero Angus McMillan was revisited in the pages of the mainstream press. Angus McMillan, the Scottish explorer, has been honoured throughout the Gippsland region. His name appears on over eighteen monuments. Many monuments are in the form of plaques on stone cairns, a nod to McMillan's Scottish Highland and Skye heritage. His face appears on a plaque at the Gippsland Immigration Park too. A prominent pastoralist and explorer, he is widely considered a key figure in the colonisation of Gippsland. In an alternative narrative, he is also known as the 'Butcher of Gippsland' for his role in leading several massacres against local Indigenous populations in the early 1840s, beginning with the attack on the Brataualung clan camped at Warrigal Creek following the murder of Ronald Macalister in 1843.[88] His leadership of a group of Scotsmen enacting violent reprisals was detailed in his letters and diaries, as well as local

[84] Julie Reid and Fay Stewart-Muir, 'I Want to Teach Aboriginal Perspectives But I Don't Want to Offend Anyone', *Victorian Curriculum and Assessment Authority*, 2017, https://www.vcaa.vic.edu.au/Documents/viccurric/proflearning/2017_Sessions/Term_2/Paralysis_of_Integrity.pptx.

[85] Ibid; Australian Heritage Commission, *Ask First: A Guide to Respecting Indigenous Heritage Places and Values* (Canberra: Australian Heritage Commission, 2002).

[86] GLAWAC, 'Annual Report 2019', https://gunaikurnai.org.au/wp-content/uploads/2019/12/GLaWAC-Annual-Report-2019-WEB-FINAL.pdf

[87] Ibid; United Nations Declaration on the Rights of Indigenous Peoples, adopted by the General Assembly in 2007.

[88] Patrick Morgan, 'Gippsland Settlers and the Kurnai Dead', *Quadrant* 48, no. 10 (2004): 26. See also Don Watson, *Caledonia Australis: Scottish Highlanders on the Frontier of Australia* (Sydney: Collins, 1984).

historical records; these stories have long been retold among descendants of both perpetrators and survivors in Gippsland. Most of the eighteen monuments to McMillan were unveiled in the 1920s as part of a broader nation-building discourse that perpetuated the myth of *terra nullius*.[89] Throughout this time, local Indigenous people, survivors of earlier conflicts in Gippsland, continued to be forcibly removed from their lands and placed in Church-run missions and then government-run reserves.[90]

McMillan's original homestead on the Avon river in West Gippsland was relocated in 1969 to the 'Old Gippstown' heritage park in Moe in the Latrobe Valley, where it remains today. Old Gippstown invites visitors to 'step back in time' to the 1850s, implying that this heritage is not packaged for Indigenous visitors. There is no mention of Indigenous histories of the area. From the 1970s onwards, the slow move towards mainstream truth telling and reconciliation butted up against this triumphal celebration of settler-explorers like McMillian. Historians provided historical accounts of genocide against Indigenous populations on the colonial frontier, and the forced removal of children from their communities and countries (the Stolen Generations).[91] Decades later, in 2008 an apology to the Stolen Generations was made in Parliament. However, the Australian government continues to debate the terms of a treaty (or treaties) with First Nations' peoples.

Despite a maturing public rhetoric, in late 2020 Wellington Shire Council voted against calls to tear down the McMillan cairns. They have not been removed despite appeals from traditional owners, led by GLAWAC, and hundreds of written community submissions. Gunai Kurnai community member Aunty Doris Paton and academics Jessica Horton and Beth Marsden wrote about the decision, calling out the council's failure to listen to Gunai Kurnai people: 'Gunaikurnai people are the experts. Gunaikurnai people know how these monuments have a deep, intergenerational impact on their community, and they shared their expert testimony with the council.'[92] As they explain, the

---

[89] Monument Australia, 'Angus McMillan Expedition', 2010, http://monumentaustralia.org.au/themes/landscape/exploration/display/30535-angus-mcmillan-expedition

[90] See Eileen Harrison and Carolyn Landon, *Black Swan: A Koorie Woman's Life* (Sydney: Allen and Unwin: 2011); Australian Broadcasting Corporation, Film Victoria Inc., and Koorie Heritage Trust, *Mission Voices* (Melbourne: ABC, 2004).

[91] For more on 1988, national memory culture and its evolution, see Tony Bennett, ed., *Celebrating the Nation: A Critical Study of Australia's Bicentenary* (Sydney: Allen and Unwin, 1992); Stephen Castles, Bill Cope, Mary Kalantzis, and Michael Morrissey, 'The Bicentenary and the Failure of Australian Nationalism', *Race & Class* 29, no. 3 (1988): 53–68; HREOC, *Bringing Them Home: Report of the National Inquiry into the Separation of Aboriginal and Torres Strait Islander Children from Their Families* (Canberra: Human Rights and Equal Opportunity Commission, 1997).

[92] Aunty Doris Paton, Jessica Horton, and Beth Marsden, 'Telling the Truth about Gippsland's History', *Overland*, 6 October 2020, https://overland.org.au/2020/10/telling-the-truth-about-gippslands-history

cairns are not a simple representation of local white-settler history; they were erected from the 1920s as part of a wider monument project, not to 'express local pride in McMillan's "discovery" ... but to consolidate a particular narrative about white settlement in the region'. They were erected by proponents of the White Australia Policy, imperialism and eugenics. GLAWAC's submission to council deals with these historical narratives, including the work the cairns do in promoting a sense of indebtedness to the deeds of pioneers in settling the region: 'the cairns represent a celebration of history where colonists arrived on Gunaikurnai land and committed forms of genocide, social engineering and legalised relocation'. They propose a process of community consultation as a path forward: 'significant and obvious actions, including pulling down or reinterpreting, must be agreed between us'. GLAWAC have been active in building a fuller picture of Gippsland's violent settler history, truths that Indigenous people have always known. But changes to AHDs are much slower, and established systems demonstrate a reluctance to accept Aboriginal voices, particularly as they pertain to the politics of sovereignty. The Wellington shire will seek the removal of some seven cairns on lands managed by other government authorities.[93]

The Gippsland Immigration Park's Heritage Trail and the Aboriginal Waterhole Creek Cultural Heritage Trail are silent on these still-simmering historical injustices. As stated, McMillan's face appears on one of the plaques at the Gippsland Immigration Park, under the label 'Migration into Gippsland'. The accompanying text, after mentioning the original inhabitants of the land, uncritically lists McMillian alongside other 'explorers' in the region, collapsing all immigrants into one category: 'The original inhabitants of Gippsland, the Kurnai Aboriginal people, have lived in this region for 20,000 years. They numbered about 4,000 when the first Europeans entered Gippsland around 1840. The explorers were mainly Highland Scots, led by Angus McMillan, as well as the Polish Count Strzelecki.'[94]

Deploying a simplistic politics of representation at heritage sites can impede nuance and mutual understanding, especially if representations are 'add-ons' to existing content, a process that mirrors the integrationist impetus of some framings of a politics of recognition. The broad application of an unreflexive white lens that obscures Black voices and stories is structural and systemic. Such muted histories confound Aboriginal efforts at truth telling; they also confound white-settler heritage consumers' capacity to respond to and engage

---

[93] Benjamin Preiss, 'Gippsland Council Rejects Call to Tear Down Monuments to Notorious Pastoralist', *The Age*, 16 June 2020, www.theage.com.au/national/victoria/voice-to-make-change-gippsland-council-to-vote-on-monument-removal-20200616-p5531r.html

[94] Gippsland Immigration Park Committee, 'Gippsland Immigration Wall of Recognition'.

Figure 3 'Migration into Gippsland' plaque from the Gippsland Immigration Park (photo taken by the author)

with such truths around dispossession and occupation, including non-Anglo migrant occupation of country. The flow-on effect of this muted cultural heritage is material: the hindered capacity of heritage management practices to draw from people's own contemporary experiences of Gunai Kurnai land (and thus the ways that country can host multiple perspectives and multiple voices) is mirrored in the continual denial of Indigenous political aspirations for treaty and an agreement with the Australian Parliament.

Despite the silences at both heritage trails, we can approach them analytically as multivocal and collaborative efforts that are open to the inscription of many truths. They *potentiate* other memories and narrative encounters associated with social justice issues. They also represent a broader push to redress Australia's collective silence on Indigenous heritage. Although this commemorative push has become highly bureaucratised and therefore sanitised and depoliticised in some instances, it marks a departure from earlier heritage exclusions.

In What Follows

I've chosen to structure this Element loosely around the historic themes that emerge from component parts of the Park. Section 2 explains the genesis of the Park, before focussing on the figure that rests at its centre: the Statue, which is also a platform to explore autobiographical histories of single migrant men in the Latrobe Valley. In exploring the perspective of the male migrant worker – the subjectivity most privileged at the Park – Section 2 provides an intimate approach to understanding regional labour and migrant histories in the post-war era. Section 3 will also unpack this subjectivity, but has a broader canvas. It will consider the intertwined industrial, deindustrial, and migrant workers' histories depicted on the Park's storyboard plaques, the nostalgia that compels this engagement with the past, and the contested resonance of coal in the heritage landscape of the Latrobe Valley today.

In reading the migrant and working-class histories associated with the Park, and considering the memories that now circulate, we need to be cognizant of the interrelationship between labour, industry, class, money, and power, as well as gender, ethnicity, and race. In official local histories, immigration and settlement into the region by Other peoples (coded in Australia as non-Anglophone) appear as a one-off aberration residing in the post-war boom period, and without lasting social, cultural, and economic impacts on the region and its heritage. The Gippsland Immigration Park, erected in 2007, entered this space and offered a counter-narrative that is rare in regional Australia. For international readers, this case study analysis and its conceptual frameworks are offered as means to pose broader questions about how communities tell their migration pasts, and how we might read these pasts with a more equitable future in mind.

The images and narratives on offer at the Park, and the language associated with its promotion, are varied. They focus not just on the sacrifices of the migrant or the journey of migration and arrival, but also on the work endured in the Valley, and the separate but linked communities of interest, work, and ethnicity that were built from these waves of migration. Accordingly, the Gippsland Immigration Park does not fit easily into the definition of monument or memorial. The Park commemorates and draws attention to industrial loss and working-class experiences as much as it celebrates and ascribes a nostalgic 'dignity' to these experiences. It also commemorates migrants (rather than migration), and a particular version of the region's working life. As a multivocal space, the Park is reflective of the various processes, negotiations, and voices involved in its creation over the last twenty or so years. Despite its political limitations, these grassroots migrant claims to history, and the politics of recognition they espouse, can be progressive in their dismissal of statist narratives of multiculturalism. Instead of reading the Park as a multicultural symbolic realm in which diversity is depoliticised and celebrated, I want to suggest that the Park can facilitate layered histories of labour and industry that challenge celebratory tropes around state multiculturalism and national progress. This work therefore tells histories that highlight historical inequalities and the effects of government stipulations or neglect on migrant and working-class lives, alongside stories of their intimate realities and ways of living within the industrial landscape of the Latrobe Valley.

2 Intimate Histories of Mobility and Labour in the Latrobe Valley: The Single Male Migrant

The Gippsland Immigration Park centres the male subject. This category of subject, however, is also laying claim to the category of Other, cultivating a subjectivity that is also migrant and working class, and therefore subject to interdependent structural discriminations. The following sections will unpack this subjectivity and its historicity in regional post-war Australia. Focussing on the experiences of the male migrant worker, this section argues that collective and public histories pertaining to this subject are more complex than celebratory state multiculturalism would have us believe. It argues that the intimate and working lives of migrant men in post-war Australia are defined by uncertainty and insecurity. In the face of structural intransience and discrimination, migrant subjects demonstrate adaptability and complex deployments of their difference in an Anglophone Australia. Here, the Park is

Figure 4 Gippsland Immigration Park seen from the 'Port of Arrival', looking
out to Princes Drive (photo taken by the author)

a springboard for telling alternative narrative histories about the Valley that
intersect working class and migrant histories. The narratives of this section are
also tied up in the biography of the main 'memory activist' behind the Park,
Don Di Fabrizio – the male migrant worker whose historic subjectivity was
arguably the model for the Park's central structure, the statue.

The Committee and Forming the Park

The Gippsland Immigration Park was officially launched in March 2007, but the
Committee behind its creation has a longer genesis. In 2003, the Italian-Australian
Co-ordinating Committee for Gippsland – consisting of local small-business

owners, school teachers, and interested individuals with an Italian heritage – expressed a desire to build a monument that would physically and symbolically represent the migrants who had come to the region. The idea was spearheaded by member Don Di Fabrizio, who formed a sub-committee that included local historian and accountant Graham Goulding, and Morwell locals Sergio and Maggie Auciello, who migrated to Australia from Italy as children.

The original idea for the monument was to 'give recognition' to Italian migrants for their 'achievements and their contribution to the region's development'.[95] But as discussions progressed within the sub-committee, a strong feeling emerged that all immigrants, and not just Italian-speaking arrivals, should be recognised. They renamed themselves the Gippsland Immigration Park Committee and proceeded to gain support from immigrant community organisations, businesses and prominent families in the Gippsland region, and Gippsland Multicultural Services. The design decisions were made by the Committee. As a small community-formed group, they did not have the funds at their disposal to conduct lengthy community consultations or survey work. The personalities and personal histories of Committee members propelled many of the design choices, as the subsequent discussion will show. Graham Goulding neatly summarises the Park's realisation, specifically the Wall of Recognition:

> So the Gippsland Immigration Wall of Recognition was built at Kernot Lake in Morwell in a parkland setting. Individuals could have their name inscribed on a granite wall with date of arrival and country of origin. A flag for each country so named would be placed in the concrete base around the monument. The wall itself comprises five separate granite walls in a semicircle with a statue in the centre representing the immigrants who came. A deck over the edge of the lake represents the port of arrival since so many arrived by ship. On the inner side of the granite walls are large bronze plaques which tell the immigrant story. The Wall of Recognition was completed and opened in March 2007.[96]

This description belies how the Park was formed over time as a physical expression of evolving relationships, one-off contributions from local businesses, and small government grants. As a result, different parts of the Park (the statue, the wall, the plaques, the flags, and the 'symbolic port' extending over the lake) do different memory work. They also appeal to different memorial traditions. And although they all reflect aspects of the region's migrant and industrial history, there is no one metaphor or emotion that moves the visitor through all elements of the Park.

---

[95] Gippsland Immigration Park Committee response to initial survey, 'Personal Correspondence', 4 August 2017.
[96] Ibid.

Locating the Park

In 2005, the Committee secured approval from the council to use the unkempt parklands around the Kernot Lake located off Princes Drive, one of the main roads through the town of Morwell. Don described the area before the Park's construction as containing 'nothing, a swamp, weeds, a paddock'.[97] As discussed in the previous section, these lands were on Gunai Kurnai country, whose people used local plants around the Waterhole Creek catchment to supplement their diets, for medicinal purposes, and to weave baskets. The Waterhole Creek Aboriginal Trail, approximately 6 km from the Park, features a 'bush tucker garden' that contains more than twenty-seven specific native plants that play an important role in the well-being of the Gunai Kurnai people. None of this knowledge was integrated into the design of the Park. As discussed in Section 1, it's an aspect of the Park that also hints at the limits of an assimilatory politics of recognition.

Princes Drive is a busy road. The location is worth exploring, as it reflects the relative public value attached to the Park and the power structures that determine the placement and heritage valuation of similar commemorative sites. The area around Kernot Lake was an available space for their ambitious project, and it afforded some visibility from the passing traffic. Notably, the Park is not located in the historic centre of the town of Morwell, along Commercial Road, which is a few kilometres south-west from the Park. This stretch includes the Morwell Centenary Rose Garden, civic offices, and the Latrobe Regional Gallery. This stretch of road and the surrounding suburban streets are older, more heavily developed areas. They are also reserved for heritage related to white European settlement before the 1920s, that is, before coal mining really took off in the Latrobe Valley. Heritage fact files and historical walks produced by the Morwell Historical Society from the early 2000s direct visitors to Commercial Road Primary School (established 1879), various protestant churches built through the late nineteenth and early twentieth centuries, Morwell Hotel and Post Office (built 1892), Masonic Hall (1927), Morwell Town Hall (built 1936), and Court House (built 1955).[98] Such sites reflect the mainstream fixation on tangible heritage as static and aesthetic, white-settler heritage structures that are categorised and canonised as authorised heritage.

---

[97] Don Di Fabrizio, 'Author's Interview with the Committee', 7 February 2018.

[98] Stephen Hellings, *Heritage Fact File: A Brief Look at Some Dates Names and Events* (Morwell: Morwell Historical Society, 2001); Stephen Hellings, *Footsteps through Time: A Heritage Walk Depicting the Morwell of Yester-Year* (Morwell: Morwell Historical Society, 2001); Stephen Hellings, *Morwell: Memories and Milestones* (Morwell: Morwell Historical Society, 1999); Debbie Edwards, *Morwell, a Historical Walk* (Victoria: D. Edwards, 1993).

While the Latrobe Regional Gallery has hosted works that showcase the region's industrial might as cultural heritage (including the 2020 Exhibition 'Electric'), the official lauding of industrial (or indeed migrant) histories is negligible.[99] The mainstream heritage trails of Morwell ignore the industrial heritage of the Valley, those visible scars on the landscape that will be explored more fully in Section 3. Layered uses of places and their migrant and working-class associations do not form part of the narrative of those places recognised as white-settler heritage. This is evident in Morwell, and across all listed heritage places in Australia.[100]

Rather than struggle to gain heritage recognition for existing structures in Morwell that may have had deep and layered migrant associations, the Gippsland Immigration Park Committee chose to build a new heritage place, one which recognises a migrant past that intersects with the region's industrial heritage.[101] Gippsland Immigration Park can be approached, therefore, as an attempt to insert the migrant and working-class perspective into mainstream heritage – to make it tangible and visible, albeit somewhat to the periphery. It is an addendum, and therefore an accurate reflection of the functioning of Australian multiculturalism.

Since the Park opened in 2007, the area around Kernot Lake has been revitalised. The council now touts the spot as a local gathering place, and it is booked for community events throughout the year. The area features a playground, barbeques and picnic tables, and a shelter on a raised platform that extends over the lake. The latter is intended to replicate a 'port, where so many immigrants began their life in Australia', and often functions as a stage for public events.[102] The Committee wished for the Park to become a communal meeting space, and not just a quiet site for reflection. As the Committee put it to me in 2019, 'the Maltese are doing their own [event] in February at the Park. Other things are happening to, other festivals. Philippines have a day. Indonesian too. Every year. The Park is used all the time'.[103] When I visited, it was a quiet spring day, and the Committee members and I were able to sit at one of the picnic tables by the lakeside and chat for hours without interruption. The Park also includes the traditional memorial element of a rose garden, which

---

[99] See Latrobe Regional Gallery, 'Electric' exhibition, 2020–2021, and exhibitions of Mandy Martin's artwork in 2019, 'Which Way the Wind Blows', which included oil paintings of APM, Loy Yang, Morwell Briquette works, https://latroberegionalgallery.com/art-trail-electric/

[100] Australian Heritage Strategy, Commissioned Essays, 'Damien Bell and Joy Elley, "Whose Heritage?"' 2011, www.environment.gov.au/heritage/australian-heritage-strategy/past-consultation/comissioned-essays

[101] Dellios, 'Migration Parks and Monuments to Multiculturalism', 25.

[102] Gippsland Immigration Park Committee, 'Gippsland Immigration Wall of Recognition'.

[103] Di Fabrizio, 'Author's Interview with the Committee'.

rings the Walls of Recognition and the storyboard plaques with their depictions of lost industrial sites.

Gaining Heritage Grants: Multiculturalism and Cultural Capital

Each component of the Park was formulated by the Committee and achieved over the years through competitive grants awarded from state and national schemes for heritage and conservation works, or for activities promoting state multiculturalism and social inclusion. Sergio Auciello's account indicates that the Committee was eventually able to use a state-sanctioned language around multiculturalism to its advantage when applying for certain grants:

> At that time, they [Victorian heritage grant bodies] were funding more things to do with heritage buildings and restoration. Out of all of this, after that, there's been a movement to multiculturalism and through the multicultural department, we have got funding since then, on different projects, little ones. The enhancements to the area, this part of it here [park benches and tables], is migration, multiculturalism, right here. Anything we did to improve that fitted in with their criteria.[104]

Due to a lack of consistent funding, maintenance works at the Gippsland Immigration Park are premised on one-off grants, like many heritage projects across the country. The Committee has not always been successful in gaining grants, in which case, it has made appeals to individual politicians (across both major political parties), strategically deploying a celebratory and bipartisan multiculturalism in its appeals. For example, the aforementioned port extending over the lake (or the 'Piazza Project') was made possible by state government grants, and Labor MP Robin Scott (Victorian Minister for Multicultural Affairs) officially opened it in September 2015.

Arguably, the Committee's pathway to cultural recognition is easier than that faced by other racialised and Indigenous peoples in Australia due to their proximity to the shifting definitions of whiteness in Australia. The largest grants for constructing the Park came from the Department of Victorian Communities and the Victorian State Multicultural Commission, the gaining of which could be attributed to the group's cultural capital. Not all communities have this cultural capital at their disposal. Access to many mainstream cultural institutions within Australia remain cut off to people from a 'Non-English-Speaking-Background'. Institutions do not accommodate the linguistic diversity of the population, and this is part of the reason why a politics of recognition can still be a radical social agenda for marginalised groups. In the case of the Committee, Goulding was an asset:

---

[104] Sergio Auciello, 'Author's Interview with the Committee', 7 February 2018.

Figure 5 The Gippsland Immigration Park's 'Piazza Project' and port extending over Kernot Lake (photo taken by the author)

a professional Anglo-Australian male, the only member without an Italian-language background. At one point in our discussions, Don lamented to me his inability to move forward at a faster pace because of his difficulties with written English and therefore with grant applications, and his reliance on others for help negotiating the government bureaucracy involved. However, Italianità has been celebrated as a key part of Australian multiculturalism since the 1970s, most visibly through the Anglophone consumption of stereotypically Italian foods. Evolving cultural processes of ethnicisation have transformed the racial and ethnic status of Italian-background peoples in Australia.[105] The Committee's Italianness was valuable cultural capital; it assisted in their gaining grants targeted at 'multi-cultural' communities. Alongside Greek-speaking migrants, Italian-speaking migrants and their social mobility have been lauded by politicians and the media as an example of the 'migrant success story'. Of course, this ignores many of the past and ongoing structural inequities that some face, in addition to the continued paucity of non-Anglophone representation in Australian politics. Furthermore, labouring the point of relative cultural capital (and hierarchies of oppression) risks ignoring the conditional integration of ethnicised peoples into the Australian body

---

[105] See Franceso Ricatti, *Italians in Australia: History, Memory, Identity* (New York: Springer, 2018).

Figure 6 Surrounds/facilities at the Park (photo taken by the author)

politic. Implicated in those processes of conditional integration (and the *mis*recognition of ethnic peoples' cultural heritage) is a deeper history of structural discrimination. These histories of structural discrimination are inextricably tied to the histories of migrant labour offered at the Park. Centring minority ethnic groups and their encounters with work and life in the Valley constitutes an intervention into a whitewashed and Anglophone public history that relies on a politics of recognition to make its intervention.

Migration and Walls

The Park's Wall of Recognition takes its cues from similar commemorative walls across Australia to migrants and immigration. When I asked Don about the initial idea behind the Park, he explained how he had travelled around Australia seeking ideas. He went to Albury-Wodonga on the New South Wales–Victoria border and visited the heritage park at the former Bonegilla Immigration Reception Centre. He also visited the Immigration Museum in Melbourne with its Tribute Walls, the Adelaide Migration Museum's Migration Memorial Wall featuring plaques erected by some of South Australia's migrant and refugee communities, and of course the Maritime Museum and its Welcome Wall in Sydney's Darling Harbour. The Sydney Welcome Wall, as public spectacle, seeks to include migrants in a narrative of nation-building. It also signals Australia as a place of welcome, in much the same way that Ellis Island's American Immigrant Wall of Honor does.[106] The latter lauds state-endorsed values of liberty and freedom afforded to those allowed entry. It was Don's visit to Ellis Island in 2006 that inspired him most. What he liked was the way families were able to easily identify their ancestors' names. The American Immigrant Wall of Honor contains over 600,000 names. It is one of New York's most popular tourist attractions. Oral historian Michael Frisch argues that people visit sites like Ellis Island with a 'sense of what is appropriate to the dignity and stature of major commemorations'.[107] Don was awed by this feeling of dignity and stature. He also told me that he felt the random way in which names were inscribed at Melbourne's Immigration Museum did not facilitate a familial and generational connection, didn't offer a time either, in which to 'place' one's ancestors in history. Don was therefore seeking to create something that would both incite awe and facilitate intimate connections with the past on a personal scale.

The Wall is a politically charged symbol that politicians draw on to indicate exclusivity, security, and protection from undesirable others, those who are framed as posing a threat to the internal (and racial) harmony of the citizenry of the nation state. Walls can be borders, stopping and redirecting free movement; but they can also contain and imprison. Conversely, they can symbolise resistance and survival. The connotations associated with walls implicate the power of larger institutions. Inscriptions *on* walls, therefore, highlight the subjectivities of individuals contained, excluded or redirected by such walls. They are a slate for marking one's place in time and space. Depending on historical context, on prevailing racial and class constraints, which side of a wall you are on can determine access to paid employment, healthcare, justice, security, and education. Borders, unlike the physical wall, can also 'follow' some people across time and space, shaping their legal and personal identities.[108] The borders of the nation state are complex institutions that are more than just physical boundaries. They are a historic means of control, inclusion, and exclusion for undesirable bodies.[109]

---

[106] See Michael Frisch, *A Shared Authority: Essays on the Craft and Meaning of Oral and Public History* (New York: State University of New York Press, 1990), 216.

[107] Ibid., 217.

[108] For more on borders and the field of border studies, see Alena Pfoser, 'Memory and Everyday Borderwork: Understanding Border Temporalities', *Geopolitics* (2020): 1–18; Liam O'Dowd, 'From a "Borderless World" to a "World of Borders": "Bringing History Back in"', *Environment and Planning D: Society & Space* 28, no. 6 (2010): 1031–1050.

[109] See Giorgio Agamben, *Homo Sacer: Sovereign Power and Bare Life.* (Stanford: Stanford University Press, 1998).

Studies in archaeology approach walls and their markings as sites requiring physical conservation. Byrne has critiqued the 'antiquarian artefact hunting' prevalent in archaeological practice as lacking empathy, specifically the empathy required to make connections with the past and the individuality of past subjects:

> Why is it, though, that we archaeologists seem mostly unable through our 'art' to evoke the individual humanity of the makers, owners and users of the artefacts we handle? ... The answer seems to lie in a whole tradition of Western science that has worked to exclude from the act of science the subjectivity of the scientist. (Latour 1993)[110]

How we tangibly map the intangible should be informed by a historical empathy that is able to account for the positionality of past subjects. As Bryne argues, 'the "lateral" connectivity entailed in this cosmopolitanism is not possible, I suggest, without a comparable ability to connect "vertically" with the community of past others'.[111] At the Gippsland Immigration Park, we are dealing with a different type of wall, one constructed as a monument and memorial to past lives, rather than the subject of archaeological hunting. But Byrne's point about historical connectivity prevails: the Park's walls are here approached for their ability to foster a sense of connectivity with the historicised migrant subject.

Despite the loaded metaphor, Australia's walls to migration are institutionally supported monuments, drawing on an AHD that creates, according to public historian Paul Ashton, a glossy Australian history that presents the nation state as a 'fair and open society'.[112] Ashton believes a 'conservative revisionist' ideology of multiculturalism rests at the centre of these acts of commemoration, which stress progress and silence instances of structural disadvantage. In contrast to spontaneous examples of community-led 'participatory memorialisation', Ashton and Paula Hamilton label such walls as an example of 'retrospective commemoration'.[113] However, state-sanctioned memories do not erase the existence of other local, familial, and ethnic processes of memory making. For example, Ashton points to migrants who choose to 'collaborate' with officially endorsed and revisionist versions of the history of the Snowy Mountains Hydro

---

[110] Byrne, 'A Critique of Unfeeling Heritage', 245; Peter Hobbins, Ursula Frederick, and Anne Clarke, *Stories from the Sandstone: Quarantine Inscriptions from Australia's Immigrant Past* (Sydney: Arbon, 2017) is a notable exception in the field of archaeology and heritage.

[111] Byrne, 'A Critique of Unfeeling Heritage', 249.

[112] Paul Ashton, '"The Birthplace of Australian Multiculturalism?" Retrospective Commemoration, Participatory Memorialisation and Official Heritage', *International Journal of Heritage Studies* 15, no. 5 (2009): 394.

[113] Paul Ashton, Paula Hamilton, and Rose E. Searby, *Places of the Heart: Memorials in Australia* (Sydney: Australian Scholarly Publishing, 2012).

Electric Scheme as a 'birthplace of multiculturalism' and a symbol of 'unity in diversity', instead of a history marred by racial tension and government containment and control.[114] In order to avoid dichotomising these collective memories into official and unofficial, it is important to remember than many migrants and their descendants in Australia participate actively in these state-endorsed acts of 'recognition': paying hundreds of dollars to have their family names inscribed on these walls. Nonetheless, the people implicated in these collective memory processes are still able to hold alternative or oppositional narratives of multiculturalism themselves, premised on lived experiences of structural inequality and racial discrimination, even as they willingly participate in some of the more superficial tenants of Australia's multiculturalism.

These are complex and ambivalent processes that cannot be easily summarised through one term or another – as participatory memorialisation or retrospective commemoration. There are both kernels of resistance to the state co-option of migrant heritage and its revisionist tendencies, and a degree of complicity in such narratives – most notably in the celebration of individual migrant success stories for those who have achieved social mobility. The Gippsland Immigration Wall of Recognition speaks to some of these tropes too, but it is less monumental than the Maritime Museum's 'Welcome Wall', despite some of Don's aspirations. It also works on a specific local and regional historical scale that this Element will unpack.

The seven granite walls of the Park are set in a semicircle: four walls are dedicated to telling the industrial and immigrant experience of Gippsland (covered in Section 3), while the remaining three walls (both sides) are made available for the inscription of names 'for those that immigrated to Australia and worked and lived in Gippsland'.[115] By the end of 2006, over 700 people paid $150 each to have their names inscribed on the walls. The names are grouped together according to the year in which they were inscribed, beginning in 2007. The family name, country of origin, and year of (first) immigration to Gippsland is listed. Each year since, the Committee hosts a ceremony for the inscription of new names on the wall. There is only a finite amount of blank wall space left, so eventually this will become a more static feature of the overall Park. For now, it functions as a unique community-building exercise, and a way to successively expand the politics of recognition to new Others, racialised and ethnicised peoples in Gippsland. For example, the Committee made note of the increasing incidence of Filipino names on the wall.[116] These are individuals who may have been residents in the Latrobe Valley for a long time, but who have only recently

---

[114] Ashton, 'The Birthplace of Australian Multiculturalism', 387.

[115] Gippsland Immigration Park Committee, 'Gippsland Immigration Wall of Recognition'.

[116] Project Management Group, 'Author's Interview with the Committee', 7 February 2018.

Figure 7 The Wall of Recognition – names on one of the walls (photo taken by the author)

felt able to make a claim to this expanding commemorative and celebratory space. The Souvenir Booklet from 2007 also mentions the Asian students coming to Monash University (now the Federation University), and 'small influxes of Russians, Chinese, Europeans and South Americans' in the 1990s, as well as the most recent wave of Sudanese refugees from the 2000s.[117] The booklet does not delve into the respective political turmoil that compelled these different groups to migrate, or how they came to settle in Gippsland specifically.

---

[117] Gippsland Immigration Park Committee, 'Gippsland Immigration Wall of Recognition'.

Some of the names on the walls are of migrants who have moved into and out of the region, and may no longer be living in Gippsland, or even in Australia. In the late 1960s, rates of return migration to Italy and the Netherlands began to exceed immigration, which some historians have attributed to poor work and living standards for non-English-speaking migrants in Australia.[118] The Gippsland Immigration Park Committee was clear that these names needed to be included too, for this experience reflected the reality of twentieth-century mobility, especially for those displaced by temporary conflict, undertaking work contracts, or not able or willing to acquire permanent settlement. It is note-worthy, and reflective of this historical experience, that some of the names that appear on the walls are of individuals who did not 'settle' in Gippsland but moved on to other parts of Australia or overseas. The thing that binds these names together is their presence (but not necessarily permanent settlement) as migrants in the Gippsland region, their being migrant. In this being migrant, successive generations make clear connections to the influence of the local power stations over their migration journeys – of the inextricable confluence between labour markets and human mobility within, in, and out of the Latrobe Valley. The Committee was particularly sensitive to the continued mobility assisted migrants experienced under their two-year work contracts with the Australian Commonwealth during the post–WWII era (1947–1972). This was the experience of Don as well as the fathers of other members of the Gippsland Immigration Park Committee.

Don Di Fabrizio: Biographical Histories of the Latrobe Valley's 'Golden Age'

The Statue

The remainder of this section will consider the historical work undertaken by the Park's statue, especially in relation to the male migrant worker and historical narratives of precarity/security. As with the walls, the idea for the statue came about through the vision of Don Di Fabrizio, the Director of the Committee. Don was born in the village of Lama Dei Peligni in the Abruzzo region of Italy in 1933. He remembers his childhood as 'hard and depressing' and has vivid memories of the Nazi occupation of his village. Don worked as a farm labourer to help support his extended family, all of whom also 'worked the fields' surrounding their village home. They were 'struggling to survive'.[119] At the

---

[118] Stephen Castles, 'Italians in Australia: The Impact of a Recent Migration on the Culture and Society of a Postcolonial Nation', *Center for Migration Studies Special Issue* 11, no. 3 (1994): 346.

[119] Donato Di Fabrizio, 'Donato Di Fabrizio – Australia', in ed. Monica Palozzi, *Le 1001 storie degli Italiani nel Mondo* (Athens: Pragmata, 2018), 150.

Figure 8 The statue at the centre of the Gippsland Immigration Park (photo taken by the author)

age of twenty, he decided to follow his older brother Giuseppe and apply for assisted passage to Australia.

At first glance, the statue seems to adhere to the positivist, triumphalist tradition of the monument. Cast in bronze, the 2-m figurative sculpture is of a 'healthy young immigrant [male] worker' on a raised dais.[120] At Don's insistence, the statue was constructed in the traditional method by artist William Eicholtz from his Melbourne studio. A short poem is inscribed on the platform under the figure, with the words 'The Migrant' most visible. The statue rests at the centre of the park, hedged by the Walls of Recognition. The young

---

[120] Di Fabrizio, 'Author's Interview with the Committee'.

man is clutching a bag, a suitcase rests at his feet, and he is shielding his eyes from the sun with his passport as he looks out to the horizon. His garb is 1950s vintage. His expression is unreadable; he is neither pleased nor upset.[121]

I see the statue as a means to link the amorphous symbolism of the walls to a specific historical experience. I spoke with the Committee about their thoughts behind its inception. The discussion came around to the representativeness of the statue and the subjective historical experiences to which it refers:

Maggie: We had to decide, would we have a family, would we have a man and a woman, or would we have a man? So then we just decided the man representing the whole family.

Serge: [A]nd that era was when most of the migration occur, post-second world war, majority came then, and the majority usually came as sole migrants, the men, and then the family came later. In that regard, it represents the majority.

Don: [The male] came here first, then they brought the family. They only brought the men here for two years contract, and they could have gone home or stayed here.

Author: and there's no indication [from his stance] that he's staying. He's looking into the distance.

Don: Well the hand like this [to his head] is two things. The first, it's because we don't want any vandals to break the hand. It's attached there. But also, the sun of Australia, from the sun, and you look on the horizon, 'where am I going?'[122]

When I asked about modelling the features of the male statue, hinting at his *de-*ethnicisation in an Anglophone Australia, Serge argued that he 'could've easily been modelled to look a way'. Don explained, in a somewhat reductionist fashion, that he 'could've been a Greek, could've been an Italian, could've been a German, actually the original one was a little bit more like a German, but then we changed it'. I am unclear what Don means here, but the implication is his origins are intended to be ambiguous. It's clear he is of continental European origin. He is white, and therefore not representative of all migrants to the region or all names inscribed on the wall, especially those arriving from the 1970s after the official abolition of the White Australia Policy. As the Committee discusses earlier, they made a choice, with the statue at least, to speak to a specific historical context and to their familial histories of post–WWII migration to Australia from Southern and Eastern Europe.

---

[121] Dellios, 'Migration Parks and Monuments to Multiculturalism', 18.

[122] Project Management Group, 'Author's Interview with the Committee'.

In some ways, the statue declines to engage in debates about the role of ethnicity and race in shaping and constraining migrants' settlement experiences (both long term and short term). It does this in the same way it ignores wider racial justice issues associated with the dispossession of Indigenous land. But its visual depictions sideline ethnicity while also centring the subjectivity of the male migrant worker and his working-class status. As I will argue in subsequent sections, this can be seen as a balm for the state-sanctioned celebratory and superficial elements of food-and-folklore multiculturalism that reify ethnicity. There are no noticeable 'ethnic markers' at the Gippsland Immigration Park.

I decline to read the concrete footpath of nation state flags that ring one side of the walls as ethnic markers, given the internal diversity and political acts of ethnic subjugation within many of those nation states. The addition of these flags to the overall Park align with a bureaucratic language around 'inclusion' that operates under the erroneous assumption that other nations, outside Australia, are internally homogeneous, and only when they come 'here' do they become multicultural. The flags also work to present the region as 'international', in addition to pre-empting any accusations of exclusivity that the statue might evoke. However, a historically specific reading of the Park, offered in subsequent sections, reveals its potential as a springboard for historical engagement with the influence of structural disadvantage on the migration and settlement experiences of a specific cohort (mainly male, Eastern and Southern European, and working class).

The Politics of Multiculturalism: Nostalgia and Class

As outlined in the Introduction, Australia's neoliberal and conservative multiculturalism has the effect of denuding considerations of the structural inequality built into past and present systems of immigration. Ghassan Hage has explored the role of 'white cosmospolitates' in this multiculturalism, in which non-Anglo people are ethnicised in a process that renders them consumable by those in positions of more power, white cosmospolitates, who may broadly ascribe to a left-leaning liberal agenda.[123] I found author Christos Tsiolkas' take on the historicity of these categories – and what has happened to perceptions of the working-class, post–WWII migrant in Australia since the decline of social justice agendas and the rise of neo-liberalism – helpful in framing my understanding of the particular politics of recognition occurring at the Park:

---

[123] Hage, *White Nation*, 201.

[I]n Australia, this peasant past has been transfigured by migration to mutate into something else: the peasant became working class. That was what happened to my Greek parents arriving in Australia. Their entry was condition on their labour being exploited; in the factories and in the quarries where they worked, and in the offices and warehouses and the private homes they cleaned. Today, their adherence to being working class is also becoming nostalgic, becoming spectral. They are now swept under the rubric of being European Australians. And the pride and the strength that was once attached to the idea of being working class is being stripped away by a new form of left-wing politics prioritising identities of race and gender and sexuality over the economic relations of class. Denunded of strength and pride, understood as the atavistic and reactionary xenophobic politics fuelling right-wing populism, the once militant idea of being working class has become a ghost. This change in Australia is enormous, this uncoupling of being migrant from being working class.[124]

Here, Tsiolkas is, much like Nancy Fraser, attempting in his analytical approach to re-centre class, in relation to the diverse social movements that are now mobilised around cross-cutting axes of difference.[125] This Element's analysis of the Park also speaks to the coupling between being 'migrant' and being 'working class', one tied to the historical experiences of post–WWII Southern and Eastern European migrants. Admittedly, the place of Western European migrants (German and Dutch migrants, who made up a sizeable portion of the post-war influx of government-assisted arrivals in the 1950s) in relation to the political category of 'whiteness' is more difficult to resolve. Historically, their experiences, and their placement in the historiography, have been described as 'easier'. The assimilation of Western (and Northern) European migrants into mainstream Anglo-Australia has been discussed in terms of their willingness to forego their native languages, and in reference to the biological racism that prevailed in post-war Australia despite horrific revelations about the Holocaust.[126] But some of these assumptions around assimilation have been challenged by the writings and commemorative efforts of the second generation, who stress the insurmountable alienation and structural discrimination of being a non-British migrant in post-war Australia, coupled with the ongoing emotional labour of recovering from traumatic

---

[124] Christos Tsiolkas, 'Class, Identity, Justice: Reckoning with the Ghosts of Europe', *Griffith Review: The European Exchange* 69 (2020): 22.

[125] Fraser, 'From Redistribution to Recognition?'.

[126] Egon Kunz, *Displaced Persons: Calwell's New Australians* (Canberra: Australian National University Press, 1988); Jerzy Zubrzycki, *Settlers of the Latrobe Valley: A Sociological Study of Immigrants in the Brown Coal Industry in Australia* (Canberra: Australian National University, 1964); James Jupp, *From White Australia to Woomera: The Story of Australian Immigration* (London: Cambridge University Press, 2002).

war and internment experiences, and experiences of displacement in the wake of WWII.[127]

Like Tsiolkas' spectral working class, the names inscribed on the Park's walls and the faces etched onto its storyboard plaques (see Section 3) evoke ghosts too, those of a past industrial era. But as Tsiolkas goes on to say, questions of class today cannot be separated from colonial legacies, which created the various waves of diaspora that in turn shape Australia's past and present. The Park only hints at these connections, at the responsibility all migrants share in the dispossession of Australia's Indigenous peoples – as mentioned, herein lies the limits of its politics of recognition. Privilege and structural disadvantage do stem from a confluence 'of gender and race identity and sexuality', as well as class.[128] The burden of the analysis then compels the following question: by ignoring or collapsing categories – into 'European', or even simply 'migrant working class' – does the Park avoid harder questions in the search for a community consensus? In a desire for broad community appeal, the Park seeks to rescue some of the lost pride of the Latrobe Valley's coal-mining history while also extending the typically Anglo-centric limits of that working-class narrative.[129] As I've argued, however, its intersectional limitations do not totally eclipse the other political and potentially radical heritage work it enables.

On one level, the Park participates in a collective nostalgia for a past prior to industrial deregulation and de-unionisation, which is unpacked further in Section 3. While the Park may ignore the fault lines of race and ethnicity, gender and sexuality, the other memory work enabled by this platform does not deter from the emotional salience of the Park's enduring nostalgia, this yearning for a more communitarian regional life that has no place in modern 'flexible' workplaces. Reading intersubjectively can also be an answer to these silences.

Racialised and migrant workers remain the most disadvantaged by casualised and insecure work. Historically, racialised minorities have been most vulnerable to breakdowns in existing social systems, to economic upheaval, and to the failure of existing Anglophone systems of governance to account for difference in times of crisis and change, as recent experiences with Covid-19, especially in Melbourne's North-West, have shown.[130] In the Latrobe Valley, shifting economic patterns from the 1980s wrought a great deal of dislocation and

---

[127] Alexandra Dellios, '"It was Just You and Your Child": Single Migrant Mothers, Generational Storytelling and Australia's Migrant Heritage', *Memory Studies* 13, no. 4 (2020): 586–600.

[128] Tsiolkas, 'Class, Identity, Justice', 22–23.

[129] Eklund, 'There Needs to be Something There for People to Remember', 168–189.

[130] www.theage.com.au/national/victoria/a-city-divided-covid-19-finds-a-weakness-in-melbourne-s-social-fault-lines-20200807-p55ji2.html. A federal coordinating body to communicate Covid-19 directives to 'CALD' communities was only established in December 2020.

disaffection to 'older' working class cohorts and their alliances. But respective cohorts were affected by degrees: newer (non-Anglo) migrant arrivals, for example, were always 'the first to go', as was the case during minor economic downturns during the late 1940s and early 1950s. While food-and-folklore markers of ethnic identity are lacking in the Park, the structural disadvantages associated with respective 'fault lines of identity' and subjective experiences of deindustrialisation are present, close to the surface.

So, while it may be monumental in form, the Park's walls and statue need not be read as strictly celebratory, and therefore as only participating in a liberalist multicultural agenda. Rather, the statue draws on monumental forms (realist bronze figurative sculpture), as well as memorial tropes (the lone male, the success story), whose meanings are here subverted. It can be read instead as an ambivalent 'counter-monument'.[131] But in order to understand this memory work, it is important to return to my historical account of Don and his migrant subjectivity.

Contract Labour and the Post-war Immigration Scheme

Don arrived in Australia in 1954 under assisted passage with the Australian government as a young labourer. Consequently, for his first two years in Australia, Don was contracted to accept whatever employment was offered him by the Australian Commonwealth Employment Office. All government-assisted migrants arriving under such schemes (those not sponsored by family or ethnic welfare organisations) were subject to a two-year work contract, except for 'dependent' (married) women with children. Single mothers were not exempt. Don's older brother Giuseppe was also working off his two-year contract in Queensland. Don's youngest brother John followed them to Australia in 1956. Australia's post-war immigration programme – which was actually a number of schemes established with nation states as well as organisations like the International Refugee Organization from 1947 – initially targeted single able-bodied young men to work in heavy industry and agriculture, industries in which there were employment shortages. Across the term of their two-year work contracts with the government, migrants could be moved multiple times, according to the availability of work and accommodation, and regardless of their family situations.

Don first found himself allocated to work at the Electricity Power Transmission (EPT) in Geelong (Victoria). He had no prior experience in heavy industry, having grown up in a rural setting. The four months he worked

---

[131] Alison Atkinson-Phillips, *Survivor Memorials: Remembering Trauma and Loss in Contemporary Australia* (Perth: University of Western Australia Press, 2019), 22.

for EPT were difficult but rewarding. Don says he is proud of his transition from unskilled labourer to one skilled in steel erection and construction (although this was not necessarily what he set out to obtain when he left Italy). It shaped the rest of his working life in Australia. He recalls first being assigned work as a rigger, and thus being forced to overcome his fear of heights.

Don and his brothers arrived at a time of full employment (with the exception of temporary declines in 1949 and 1952), but not much support was offered in terms of workplace health and safety. Endless shifts and short breaks were also a notable feature of this period in Don's life. During this time, Don lived in a tent because the EPT worker's camp (of communal wooden barracks) was at full capacity. He recalls that first night 'in the little tent I was freezing. I had not been so cold since the war years'.[132] His housing situation did not improve when he moved on to his next position in the town of Morwell, where he was promised employment at the new Morwell power station and briquette factory undertaking steel erection: 'with 6 other men we were transported on the tray of an old tip truck on the 7-hour journey to our new home. Our destination was to a hill site 1 km. East of Morwell, where once again we slept in tents'.[133]

Migrant Labour and Expansion in the Latrobe Valley and Morwell

Industrialisation in the Latrobe Valley occurred rapidly from the late 1920s, and the impacts on community and regional identity were profound. As local historian Legg describes in his celebratory and civic-minded history of the region, the 'industrial monoliths and the scars of open cuts now appeared in pastures which had long been the mainstay of the Shire's economy', indicating how rapidly the cultural and natural had landscape changed.[134] Within a few years, many of the dairy farms that had expanded across unceded Indigenous lands during the nineteenth and early twentieth centuries, including the 'thick ti-tree scrub' on the southern bank of the Latrobe river, were taken over by mass industrial enterprise. This was a state-sponsored industrial development. The newly established State Electricity Commission of Victoria (SECV) re-envisioned the region from the early 1920s. The Latrobe Valley's rich brown coal deposits, and the possibility of briquette production, became Victoria's answer to a predicted growth in power needs. In the process, power production transformed how the Valley was viewed and how it viewed itself: an industrial hub, monumental in scale, both visually arresting and horrifying, cantankerous, dirty, even smelly. But it was the people who changed most of

---

[132] Di Fabrizio, 'Donato Di Fabrizio – Australia', 152.   [133] Ibid., 153.

[134] Stephen Mark Legg, *Heart of the Valley: A History of the Morwell Municipality* (Melbourne: Royal Victorian Institute for the Blind, 1995), 234.

all: a new influx of people from diverse social and cultural backgrounds, with expectations of full employment with the SECV, arrived in the Valley, Don among them.[135]

From the late 1940s, the SECV expanded beyond Yallourn into Morwell, Moe, and Traralgon, the three main towns of the Latrobe Valley. Morwell before 1945 has been described as an 'inconsequential farming town'.[136] The SECV sought to transform these towns from disjointed farming centres and railway towns into an industrial region that would provide up to 75 per cent of the state's electricity production. Morwell power station and Morwell briquette factory were constructed in the 1950s and 1960s. In Morwell in 1955, Don once again found himself living in a tent. He was charged, with a handful of other migrant men, with erecting new purpose-built wooden barracks for incoming workers, most of them assisted migrants like Don. He remembers, 'almost everyone on the job spoke Italian as they were migrants too'.[137]

Throughout the 1950s and 1960s, the Commonwealth government publicised the economic and social benefits of its mass immigration scheme, the largest influx of new arrivals the Australian nation state had ever seen. A demand for labour pushed this scheme on until the early 1970s. It was matched, however, by a severe housing shortage across the country. Australian government officials expressed the expectation that new arrivals, especially those from outside the British Isles, would accept lower standards of accommodation.[138] They were also expected to make few demands on existing social services and seamlessly assimilate into mainstream culture. The Commonwealth's approach to the emotional and familial dimensions of the immigration scheme was haphazard and ill-prepared. The assumption that new arrivals would consent to assimilate were underpinned by racist stereotypes and a belief in the superiority of 'British' stock. Political scientists Breuer and Power described the government's approach to immigration as the 'AWESOME policy ... Assist White European Settlers; Other Migrants Excluded', insisting that this remnant of the White Australia Policy continued to shape the reception afforded to continental

---

[135] The main focus of the SECV until after WWII was Yallourn Power Stations, the first of which began in 1925, accompanied by the newly constructed garden city of Yallourn, which the SECV created and administered for its workers. In 1961, the SEC announced that the town would be 'dug up for the coal that lay underneath', and this much-lauded 'visionary' planned town was demolished in the early 1970s, disappearing into an open-cut coal mine. See Meredith Fletcher, *Digging People up for Coal: A History of Yallourn* (Melbourne: Melbourne University Publishing, 2002).

[136] Tom Doig, *Hazelwood* (Melbourne: Random House Australia, 2019), 57.

[137] Di Fabrizio, 'Donato Di Fabrizio – Australia', 152.

[138] Alexandra Dellios, *Histories of Controversy: Bonegilla Migrant Centre* (Melbourne: Melbourne University Publishing, 2017), 10–25.

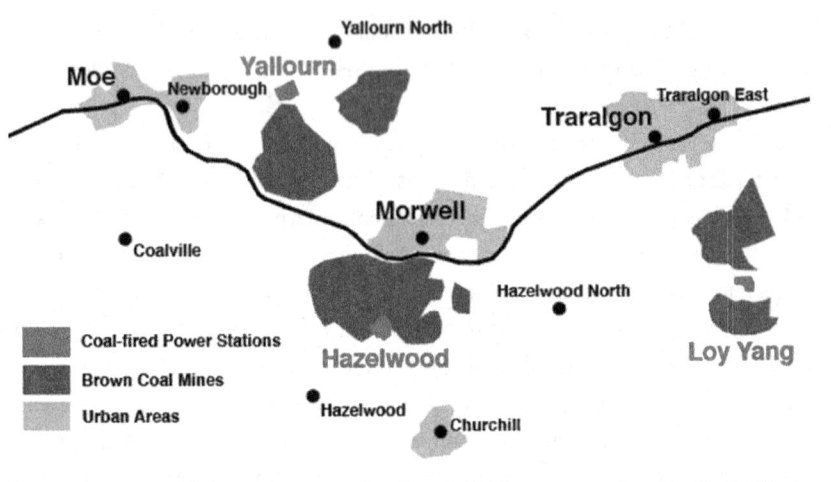

Figure 9 A map of the major towns and coal-fired power stations in the LaTrobe Valley. Map made by Nick Carson, June 2009. Permissions open, see licensing permission here: (https://commons.wikimedia.org/wiki/File: LaTrobe_Valley_CFPS.png)

European migrants from the post-war era.[139] Needless to say, many non-British arrivals found the housing situation and the terms of their work contracts difficult to navigate.[140] While industry and employment had expanded rapidly in the Latrobe Valley, housing and social services had not kept apace. This situation was compounded by restrictions placed on the expansion of residential settlements resting on or near coal-bearing land, especially to Morwell's east. Most SECV employees, especially migrant workers in Morwell, found accommodation in male-only workers' hostels and, eventually, in commission homes being built by the Victorian Housing Commission from the 1950s.

The industrial development of the region peaked in the 1950s and early 1960s, what Legg calls 'the confident years'. In addition to open-cut coal mines, the region became home to electricity generation, briquette manufacture, gasification, and paper and cement manufacture, all of which used the seemingly bountiful reserves of brown coal that had transformed the Latrobe Valley.[141] Like many others who arrived in the region during the confident years, Don remembers this era fondly. Sociologist Jerzy Zubrzycki conducted his study of immigrants to the region in this period, publishing the results in *Settlers of the Latrobe Valley: a sociological study of immigrants in the brown*

---

[139] Jeremy Bruer and John Power, 'The Changing Role of the Department of Immigration', in *The Politics of Australian Immigration*, ed. James Jupp and Marie Kabala (Canberra: Australian Government Publishing Service, 1993), 107.

[140] Ibid.   [141] Zubrzycki, *Settlers of the Latrobe Valley*, xiii.

coal industry in Australia in 1964. At the time, Zubrzycki was a proponent of assimilation, and the study was therefore interested in migrant adjustments to the so-called Australian way of life, with the onus placed on the migrant subject to adjust. Migrants were the nation's answer to manpower shortages, and unlike in Western Europe, they were not guest workers but were expected to settle and take up citizenship. As stated, while the mass immigration scheme was marketed to the Anglo-Australian population as a means to fill population growth targets, this does not mean any concessions were made for their 'absorption' into the settler-colonial state. Like their wholesale absorption into mass industry, their subjectivities were erased, and as migrant activists and commentators have argued, they were reduced to 'factory fodder'.[142] This narrative appears alongside, in ambivalent fashion, more celebratory renderings of the mass postwar immigration scheme.[143]

Zubrzycki's study made generalisations around broad ethnic categories that were perceived to affect adjustment, switching between categories like 'Southern European', and Maltese, Italian, and Greek, for example. The study produced figures for migrants' occupational adjustment, standard of living, structure of family life, and social/cultural participation. Ultimately, it lacked the longitudinal data to support some of its arguments about the 'rate of adjustment' associated with respective ethnicised groups. It also declined to seriously consider the diverse effects of pre-migration experiences (including civil war) on the structure and emotional parameters of family life in Australia. The epistemological basis of Zubrzycki's *Settlers in the Latrobe Valley* is a product of its time. The study also noted the reticence and even hostility displayed to Zubrzycki's research team by some Displaced Persons from the Baltic states, those who had fled to Western Europe after the Soviet invasion of their home states. Their reluctance to participate in the study's surveys and interviews is attributed to their suspicion and fear of surveillance, which in itself provides an indication of the nature of this cohort's emotional adjustment to Australian settlement.

Overall, the study gives a sense of the Valley's rapid population change, even if migrant voices themselves are lacking in the text. Zubrzycki noted:

> There was great activity . . . an air of prosperity, no doubt due to the enormous rate of recent expansion. Many of the immigrants and local Australians when interviewed spoke of it as the 'boom' town, recalling the years of 1955–7

---

[142] Fitzroy Ecumenical Centre Quarterly Journal *EKSTASIS*, No. 8, February 1974.

[143] Ibid.; George Zangalis, *Migrant Workers & Ethnic Communities: Their Struggles for Social Justice & Cultural Rights: The Role of Greek-Australians* (Melbourne: Common Ground, 2009).

when the construction on the SEC [State Electricity Commission] undertaking was in full swing.[144]

According to the 1961 census, a growing number of Dutch-, Italian-, German-, Maltese-, and Polish-speaking peoples were living and working in the Valley. Immigrant men and their families formed a significant proportion of the workforce in the brown coal industry. The region was identified as containing an 'unusually high concentration of overseas-born in the population, proportionately more numerous than in other comparable areas in Australia'.[145] The figures also indicated that the population was the youngest in the state of Victoria and had a higher proportion of working age men. Don and his brothers, for example, were all in their early twenties, like most of their compatriots. Accordingly, men like Don, when they were not working or attending evening English language lessons, sought opportunities to socialise. Don recalls going into Morwell town two or three nights a week to the cinema or a local dance. At one of these dances, he met his Australian-born wife, Maureen, whom he married in 1961. He conveyed to me in our conversations how grateful he'd been that Maureen spoke English to him clearly and slowly, unlike other Australians he had met.

After passing through Melbourne and Geelong on short-term work contracts, Don recognised that there was plenty of work available within the power industry in Morwell, and after meeting his wife, he made the choice to settle there permanently. Similar to Italian, Greek, Maltese, German, Polish, and other Eastern European migrants who worked in the Latrobe Valley across this period, Don arrived via a circuitous route. These movements were determined by the terms and constraints of work contracts, which did not always allow for the unification of families or the individual desires and needs of migrants. As historian Karen Agutter found, this 'continuum of mobility' faced by assisted migrants throughout the post-war period, deeply shaped these men's orientations to the landscape and their ability to form emotional attachments to place.[146] In this regard, Don's experience was not typical. Migrants' work contracts with the Commonwealth government created an 'endless parade of people being shifted from place to place' throughout the 1950s and well into the 1960s, and this description, as it applied to single working migrant men, is worth bearing in mind when reading the statue's historic subjectivity.

---

[144] Zubrzycki, *Settlers of the Latrobe Valley*, 20–22.   [145] Ibid., 33.
[146] Karen Agutter, 'Displaced Persons and the "Continuum of Mobility" in the South Australian Hostel System', in *On the Wing: Mobility before and after Emigration to Australia, Visible Immigrants*, Volume 7, ed. Margrette Kleinig and Eric Richards (Melbourne: Anchor Books, 2013), 136–152.

Historian Zora Simic's study of single non-British migrant men of this period argued that their loneliness and isolation, their cultural, linguistic, physical and social alienation, was profound. Increasing rates of return migration in the 1960s offer another indication of the situation facing transient working men. This was more than just the personal strain of migration and settlement; as Simic highlights, the cause of their misery could be 'general and structural', the result of a mass immigration scheme that produced a 'surplus of men'.[147] The situation gave rise to marriage-by-proxy, specifically among Italian migrants as the Catholic Church authorised proxy marriages. It was also matched by sporadic government attempts to balance the sexes with new migration schemes targeting young working women from Greece and Italy. The sex imbalance was especially acute for these ethnic groups, as well as the Displaced Persons from Eastern Europe who had arrived from 1949 to 1952. Simic explores the influence of assimilationist rhetoric and images of the amorphous 'Australian way of life' on this cohort. Marriage, and the formation of the nuclear family, was a key feature of media representations of successful migration and assimilation, which could 'bring to the fore issues of loneliness, isolation and despair, drawing sympathetic attention to the difficulties of settlement . . . conversely, migrant men lacking the domesticating influence of women could be perceived as threatening'.[148] The single male migrant – synonymous with 'worker' – was a ubiquitous presence in the Latrobe Valley throughout the post-war era. His existence and perceptions of his character were defined by isolation, insecurity, and transience. And this framework provides new meaning to the lone male figure at the centre of the Gippsland Immigration Park – the statue encapsulates this historic subjectivity.

Sociologist Jean Martin's more ethnographic approach to the 'integration' of Displaced Persons in Australia offers a good counter-study to Zubrzycki's Latrobe Valley study. Martin's *The Migrant Presence* was published over ten years later in 1978, when the period of assimilationist approaches to the migrant presence was coming to an end. Instead, an integrationist stance was developed by herself and other sociologists like David Cox, and eventually Zubrzycki as well, to tackle some of the obvious shortcomings of assimilation.[149] Her work considered Australian structural responses – welfare, education, health, religion, politics, and unions – to the immigrant influx, tracing the shift from a dominant

---

[147] Zora Simic, 'Bachelors of Misery and Proxy Brides: Marriage, Migration and Assimilation, 1947–1973', *History Australia* 11, no. 1 (2014): 149–174.

[148] Ibid., 154.

[149] Jean Martin, *The Migrant Presence: Australian Responses, 1947–1977* (Sydney: George Allen and Unwin, 1978).

assimilationist paradigm to a more integrationist approach that conceded migrants came with their own needs, cultural identities, and abilities to participate in civic life.

An integrationist approach placed some of the onus for adjustment on governmental structures and Australian society, rather than just the incoming migrant. As Don made clear in his written and verbal testimony, his ability to adjust and participate in Morwell's civic life was hindered by housing and work contracts, but helped by the reassuring presence of his two brothers, as well as other Italian-speaking migrants he encountered at work and play. Although it ultimately endorsed the assimilation of migrant cultures, Martin's published work also left some room for the felt ambivalence of individual arrivals, and their complex associations with Australian society, especially as it adopted a more long-standing interest in migrant adjustment over a decade-long period.

Australian structural intransigence – from government bodies and education systems, trade unions, and professions (especially regarding the dismissal of migrants' overseas qualifications) – has affected the lived experiences of migrants over a long period of time, and arguably a political intransigence has persisted. The Latrobe Valley was no different. Most migrant men, especially from Southern and Eastern Europe, entered the labour market at the lowest rungs, regardless of their past training. Zubrzycki's study noted that 'British-born settlers have the highest average weekly wage, which exceeds the lowest-paid group (Italians and Greeks) by 3 pounds 10s' in the Valley.[150] In the 1950s, this constituted a considerable wage gap. While Don did not explicitly express any grievances about his initial position within the Latrobe Valley labour force, other migrants have not been so generous, noting their exclusion from leadership positions and stalled advancement within trade union hierarchies.[151] It was ultimately what compelled Don and his brothers to leave their jobs as workers for the SECV and form their own business.

Living Ethnicity in the Valley and Post-war Clubs and Communities

As already indicated, aside from the overwhelming masculine nature of the work-force in the Latrobe Valley, there were also noticeable 'ethnic concentrations' in certain parts of the Valley, premised on prior waves of migration and the natural desire for cultural familiarity, on work availability, and on the timing and dispersal of separate migration agreements. Zubrzycki noted that single Italian men 'demonstrated a preference' for Morwell, where their numbers 'increased ninefold between

---

[150] Zubrzycki, *Settlers of the Latrobe Valley*, 91.

[151] George Zangalis, 'Our Unions or Theirs', in *Ethnic Rights, Power and Participation toward a Multi-Cultural Australia*, ed. Des Storer and Centre for Urban Research & Action (Melbourne: Clearing House on Migration Issues, Ecumenical Migration Centre and Centre for Urban Research and Action, 1975), 26.

1954 and 1960'.[152] This was due to the town's expansion into power stations from the 1950s, which occurred in conjunction with the Italian–Australian migration agreement in 1951 (halted in 1952 and then picked up again in 1954).[153] A focus on ethnic concentrations, however, obscures the interlocking and highly mobile nature of migrant labour across the Latrobe Valley, and Australia, during this time; this depended on the availability and demand for labour. Furthermore, within work, school, play, or home, people did not exist in discrete, hermetically sealed mono-ethnic spaces. Their migration journeys were defined by more than one 'arrival', as names on the wall demonstrate. Nor did they articulate, after first arriving in Australia, a stable state of pre- and post-migrancy, as Don's migration journey demonstrates.

Nevertheless, safe spaces were created within work and play out of necessity. Donat Santowiak, interviewed in 2014 as part of the Australian Generations Oral History Project held by the National Library of Australia, remembers 'lot of children from immigrant background at school [in Morwell] – particularly Italians and Greeks – but they hung together in kind of groups'.[154] Donat was born in Poland in 1950; his parents made the difficult decision to leave and migrate to Australia in 1964. He spoke German, Polish, and Russian, but was set on 'assimilating', shedding his accent, and 'becoming invisible, undetectable, verbally, physically', which is tied to his experiences of racial abuse. Donat repeatedly mentions the 'real discrimination … I mean I remember getting belted up at school … I ended up nearly losing all my teeth … being physically thrown out of shops because I couldn't pronounce the name of a particular product the way, you know, the man expected me to say it'. His response was to shed his ethnic markers, something he returned to later in life. Donat's teenage integration into the Latrobe Valley is offered as a counterpoint to Don, as a single male labourer. These negotiations, the shifting multi-ethnic spaces in which migrants and non-Anglo-Australian subjects operated, were shaped by structural and institutional constraints. And these migrant experiences are less readily accommodated by a state-sanctioned Australian multiculturalism that leaves no room for the politics of difference. Read in this context, the signifiers at the Park, like the statue, become unstable; celebration cannot be its only impetus.

Since the 1950s, Morwell has been home to active ethnically aligned clubs, such as the Italian Club, the German Club, a branch of the Greek Orthodox Community

---

[152] Zubrzycki, *Settlers of the Latrobe Valley*, 26.

[153] For more on unemployment, the Italian–Australian migration scheme, and migrant rights protests in 1952, see Dellios, *Histories of Controversy*, chapter 4, pp. 125–162.

[154] Donat Santowiak interviewed by Alistair Thomson in the Australian generations oral history project, National Library of Australia, 2014, https://nla.gov.au/nla.obj-220175608/listen

of Victoria, and the Maltese Community Centre. Donat also remembers the Polish dances his parents would attend. When considering these histories, it is important to also recall that these clubs operated as an oasis in the sometimes-hostile Anglophone landscape of the Valley, despite the strength of the migrant presence in the region. Soccer became especially important, and as an act of resistance to assimilation. A 2005 council-funded Heritage Study of the region mentions the strength of the sport owes much to Italian migration, and 'the support of the De [sic] Fabrizio brothers'.[155] The Morwell Falcons Soccer Club was formed in 1960 by newly arrived Italian migrant men living in towns across the Valley. Don became heavily involved in the running and promotion of this club in 1969, and his involvement is a point of civic pride for him. His involvement in the Falcons is a tangible melding of his local and global mindedness, built not just around ideas of 'Italianness' but on a sense of regional community identity, of being an able-bodied young migrant man in the Valley, depicted literally in the statue at the centre of the Park. The club was a gathering point, as well as an energy outlet for isolated and disenfranchised migrant men, almost all of whom worked in the local power industry. This relationship between Don and his financial and commercial resources (in the form of his company DIFABRO) and the Falcons also speaks to the Australia-wide phenomenon emerging in the post-war era: of ethnically organised clubs supported by ethnic businesses (or in some cases, by industries employing large numbers of ethnic workers).

Housing, Homes, and Family Life

The Department of Immigration deemed the temporary accommodation on offer to working men – tents, for Don – not suitable for their partners and children. They were instead accommodated in Department of Immigration 'Holding Centers' (or similar state-run hostels) established for 'dependents' of working migrant men. Former Department of Defence training camps in Greta in NSW, for example, or Benalla in VIC, were used as Holding Centres. Their location meant women and children were often miles away from their partners, who were working in large industrial projects like the Snowy Mountains Hydro Electricity Scheme, Port Kembla steelworks, or power stations and coal mines in the Latrobe Valley. A period of family separation and isolation in regional Australia was common for many working-class migrants throughout and sometimes beyond the term of their two-year work contracts with the Australian government.

Zubrzycki dedicated a section of his survey of the Latrobe Valley to 'family life', which was categorised as being 'under stress' and 'rooted in the process of

---

[155] Context Heritage Consultants, 'Latrobe City Heritage Study, Volume 1: Thematic Environmental History, Final Report 20 May 2005', Prepared for Latrobe City Council, 27–29.

migration and difficulties of adjustment'.[156] His definitions of family life are unclear here, but seem to be premised on nuclear family structures, ideas that also shaped the decisions of Australian Migration Officers placed overseas, who considered the male 'breadwinner' as the head of a family.[157] But the nuclear family was not a traditional structure for many Southern and Eastern European migrants, who often left behind extensive extended family and village networks. Through the stipulations of their work contracts, they saw their families separated across Australia according to the availability of work and accommodation. Mass industrialisation had a disorganising effect and 'mellowing influence on family life', especially for Italian and Southern European migrants from rural backgrounds.[158] Furthermore, access to and knowledge of material supports was essential for aiding migrant settlement – housing, in particular. The sense of precarity facing families was mirrored in the housing they endured in the Valley.

Don, after a period of time living in tents, eventually lived in a purpose-built camp with 100 other migrant men. He was also reunited with his two brothers, who, after also working in Geelong, joined him working in and around the Latrobe Valley by the late 1950s: 'you can imagine how happy I was to have someone from my own family with me'.[159] While living in makeshift accommodation in Morwell, the three brothers made the decision to build a home for themselves and their growing families. They built a home by sourcing construction materials from wherever they could and relying on their newly acquired skills in construction. Although all three brothers were sending money back home to their parents in Italy, as many Italian migrants did, they were able to save enough to buy a block of land in Morwell: 'We made all the concrete bricks by hand so it was slow progress as we could only work on the house on Sundays. Over the next 3 years we built a large double storey house. … Our 3 families all lived in the same house.' Building a home, often without the right construction skills and know-how, and with materials sourced from excess or discarded materials from construction sites, was common for many migrants living and working in regional areas across Australia throughout the 1950s and 1960s. The residential construction industry was little regulated at the time, and, as stated, housing was in short supply across the country. For those who wanted out of the hostel system, and hoped to be reunited with their families, erecting their own homes provided a solution. According to Don, he and his brothers built one of the

---

[156] Zubrzycki, *Settlers of the Latrobe Valley*, 113.

[157] Alexandra Dellios, 'Remembering Mum and Dad: Family History Making by Children of Eastern European Refugees', *Immigrants and Minorities: 'Special Issue: Memory and Family in Australian Refugee Histories'* 36, no. 2 (2018): 105–124. And also Ruth Balint, '"To Reunite the Dispersed Family": War, Displacement and Migration in the Tracing Files of the Australian Red Cross', *History Australia* 12, no. 2 (2015): 124–142.

[158] Zubrzycki, *Settlers of the Latrobe Valley*, 125.

[159] Di Fabrizio, 'Donato Di Fabrizio – Australia', 152.

Figure 10 Plaque nine of wall three, 'Settling In', housing and accommodation

first double storey brick homes in Morwell, using hand-made cement bricks.[160] Visitors to the Park get a sense of this industrious energy of new settlers from the storyboard plaque depictions (addressed further in Section 3) – the 'Settling In' series of storyboard plaques features images of migrants constructing their own homes, in addition to images of pre-fabricated homes in the 1950s.

Committee member Serge Auciello included a chapter about his father Giuseppe (Joe) Auciello in *Stories of the Wall,* in which he narrates the transient and difficult nature of post-war labour in Australia and finding suitable accommodation for a family.[161] Joe arrived in 1955 ahead of his family, who remained in Italy until 1959. He sent most of his wages back home to his family and to pay off debts to the Italian credit agency that had partly funded his travel to Australia. He also moved from job to job for the first few years of his work contract. The story about his settlement experience in Gippsland stresses the hard labour of these years – he worked double shifts at the power and briquette factory in Morwell, where he was transferred after working at Yallourn North Extension Mine and then Yallourn briquette factory while living in the single men's camp, like Don. Before he could request to sponsor his family for migration to Australia, however, Joe needed to find a solution to his housing situation. Like Don, he also built a house for his family in Morwell.

Donat Santowiak recalls his family's 'rude awakening' upon their arrival in Morwell. Donat arrived in Australia as a teenager in 1964 with his parents and younger sister.[162] They initially lived in the small town of Maffra in Victoria with extended family before moving to Morwell when his Dad was offered a job with the SECV. The family of four rented one room in 'the back of a house that was owned by a German lady in Morwell'. My father recounted similar stories to me: at the age of twelve, he migrated with his parents and brother from Northern Greece to South Melbourne in 1969; they too rented a single room from a migrant family who hailed from the same village in Greece. Like many Southern European migrant groups, they built a community networked by kin, region, ethnicity, and working life. They also picked up some Polish and Yugoslav dialects. In Melbourne and Sydney, migrant workers employed in factories often found shared housing in run-down and overcrowded Victorian workers' cottages in the industrial inner suburbs. It was not uncommon for an entire family to rent one room in an already overcrowded house.[163] Housing had

---

[160] Souvenir Booklet.

[161] Cited in *Stories from the Gippsland Immigration Wall of Recognition,* Volume 1, Editorial Committee (Gippsland Immigration Park Inc., 2012), 9–13.

[162] Santowiak interviewed by Thomson.

[163] Barry York, 'The Boarding Houses of 1950s Coburg', *Search: The Quarterly Journal of the Coburg Historical Society* no. 121 (December 2020); see also Mirjana Lozanovska, *Migrant Housing: Architecture, Dwelling, Migration* (London: Taylor & Francis Group, 2019), 53–56.

not kept pace with the migrant influx to the cities either. Four decades later, in the 1990s, the Bureau of Immigration and Population Research reported that migrant accommodation remained substandard, and migrants from non-English -speaking backgrounds faced systemic limitations to access and finance for appropriate housing.[164]

The first generations' residence in inner-city terrace homes was to leave little material trace once they moved out along transport lines – their occupation is generally unrecognised by heritage overlay assessments. However, Lozanovska's recent book *Migrant Housing* traces the understudied contribution of post-war migrants on the urban and architectural environment of Melbourne. She argues that Southern European migrants revitalised these 'dirty suburbs', including through 'Mediterranean insertions' on historic building stock, in addition to the more ephemeral impacts of social gatherings. From the 1970s and 1980s, these cohorts moved from suburbs like Fitzroy, Collingwood, and Carlton in Melbourne's inner north to suburbs like Lalor, Sunshine, and Thomastown in the outer north and west.[165] They sought bigger homes in newer suburbs, but they also moved in response to the decline in Australian manufacturing.

Despite their invisibility in heritage assessments of the inner-city, the early literature published from the 1970s on Southern European migrant groups tends to focus on their experiences in inner Melbourne and Sydney.[166] Regional locations in post-war Australia presented different problems for non-British migrants. In the post-war era, regional towns on or near coal-rich land were expanding into more stolen Indigenous country. Unlike in the coastal cities, regional towns contained little existing settler infrastructure – however rundown – for migrants to adopt, appropriate, and layer their settlement histories onto.

Donat's family was eventually offered a place in a new Housing Commission home, something to which SECV workers were entitled. He describes the home as 'barren' and basic; this feeling permeated his attitudes towards the social milieu of the Latrobe Valley, compounded by his violent encounters with racism in the majority Anglo-Australian community. Similarly, the Aalbers family,

---

[164] P. N. Junankar, David Pope, and Cezary Kapuschinski, *Recent Immigrants and Housing, Australian Bureau of Immigration and Population Research* (Canberra: Australian Government Publishing Service, 1993).

[165] Helen Armstrong, 'Migrant Heritage Places in Australia', *Historic Environment* 13, no. 2 (1997): 12–23.

[166] For example, Kristen Allen et al., *Greek Families in Hawthorn and Clifton Hill* (Melbourne: General Studies Department, Swinburne College of Technology, 1974); Eva Isaacs, *Greek Children in Sydney* (Canberra: Australian National University Press, 1976); David Cox, 'Greek Boys in Melbourne', in *Greeks in Australia*, ed. Charles Price (Canberra: Australian National University Press, 1975), 143–187; Gillian Bottomley, 'Community and Network in a City', in *Greeks in Australia*, ed. Charles Price (Canberra: Australian National University Press, 1975), 112–142.

who migrated from war-devastated Holland in 1956, recalled the family's initial impressions of the landscape and the housing they encountered in the Valley: 'The girls were shocked to see the dry country with houses that looked like matchboxes, unmade roads, no footpaths and outside toilets.'[167] Homes built by migrants from the 1950s, including the Fabrizio brothers' home in Morwell, had distinct 'front matter', compared to the typical detached brick veneer home. They contain elaborate front gardens, and the home is often elevated above ground level with monumental stairs, complimented by geometrically ordered concrete surfaces and gateways.[168] In short, they transformed the look and feel of many suburbs across the country, including regional centres.

I present these memories of wanting and absence *not* as a means to contrast a barren regional cultural milieu with the 'visible and distinct shaping of the built environment and urban culture' practiced by ethnics in the big cities, but rather to account for an array of cultural encounters with the idea of home and housing.[169] In both regional and urban settings, migrants had an impact on their built environments and the wider cultural habitus. Locating and commemorating their impacts is the task at hand in this heritage work, and it is neither easier nor more straightforward to identify and historicise their presence in Melbourne as opposed to Morwell.

Conclusions

In 1971, Hazelwood power station was built in East Morwell, near the open-cut mine established after WWII. Although the initial 'minimum buffer zone' between the town of Morwell and the open-cut coal mine was set at 1.6 km, this became just 400 m as the SECV continued to expand throughout the 1970s.[170] Section 3 will explore the dire social and health consequences of this expansion for residents of Morwell. Unlike other industrial centres in Western Europe and Britain, coal mining did not slow down in the Latrobe Valley from the 1970s; the SECV predicted growth beyond the 1970s, opening Yallorn W (power station) in 1973, another huge open pit (Loy Yang) in 1984, as well as power stations Loy Yang A and then B, in south-east of Morwell. Neither the state nor the federal government made any long-term plans for the transition to a post-industrial economy – the boom was expected to last.

Don and his brothers launched their own steel construction company in 1963 based in Morwell. As Don explains, 'my brother John and I saw an opportunity to earn extra money. We worked our day jobs then came home and worked in the

---

[167] Cited in *Stories from the Gippsland Immigration Wall of Recognition*, 5.

[168] Lozanovska, *Migrant Housing*, 84.   [169] Ibid., 56–57.

[170] See David Langmore, *Planning Power: The Uses and Abuses of Power in the Planning of the Latrobe Valley* (Melbourne: Australian Scholarly Publishing, 2013).

back shed making wrought iron for the many new houses that were being built to accommodate the new arrivals'.[171] The company, D & G Di Fabrizio Steel Fabrication and Erection grew rapidly throughout the 1960s, mainly taking on big contracts from the SECV. They moved to a larger factory in the 1970s as the company grew into the DIFABRO Group of companies, of which Don was the Founder and Managing Director until his retirement in 1993.

During one of our interviews in his home in Churchill, a more affluent township 10 km from Morwell, Don motioned to the now-redundant facade of Hazelwood power station and its domineering eight chimneys. He was proud to tell me that he helped build it in the 1970s. DIFABRO played a role in building the industrial landscape of the Latrobe Valley, now seen in its deteriorating industrial remains. The subsequent section will explore the mixed feelings around industrial remains, specifically Morwell and Hazelwood power stations, which have both been partially demolished in the last few years. These power stations make an appearance too on the storyboard plaques on the walls of the Park, also discussed in the next section. Don recounted his fond memories of those arduous times from his comfortable home. Ultimately, DIFABRO was broken up and its remaining factories were downgraded in the wake of the SECV's privatisation from the 1990s. Nonetheless, Don is in many ways the perfect example of the migrant success story – the one politicians love to quote and the media like to profile – a migrant entrepreneur. This 'success' is tempered by what happened to the socio-economic prospects of the Valley after privatisation, which is addressed in the following section.

In Figure 11, Don is photographed in front of the Park's statue, for a piece in the local *Latrobe Valley Express* celebrating his Latrobe City's Citizen of the Year award on Australia Day 2016.[172] 'A successful Latrobe Valley business-man', Don has been a prominent figure in his local community; his trajectory seems to fit perfectly into popular narratives about the success of post-war immigration. And his expressed gratefulness to the nation state makes him a non-threatening poster boy for more superficial and ultimately integrationist versions of multiculturalism. He 'enriches' Australia, a trope which, as Ian McShane has explored in relation to migration history in Australian museums since the 1980s, positions white Australia as consumer and agent.[173] The use of Don's narrative in popular media, the awarding of his Order of Australia Medal

---

[171] Di Fabrizio, 'Donato Di Fabrizio – Australia', 152.

[172] Gary Stevens, 'The Vision to Succeed', *Latrobe Valley Express*, 28 January 2016.

[173] Ian McShane, 'Challenging or Conventional? Migration History in Australian Museums', in *Negotiating Histories: National Museums Conference Proceedings*, ed. Darryl McIntyre and Kirsten Wehner (Canberra: National Museum of Australia, 2001), 122–133.

Figure 11 Director of the Gippsland Immigration Park Committee, Don Di Fabrizio, standing in front of the park, 2016. (photograph by Bryan Petts-Jones for *The Latrobe Valley Express*) (Used with permission, *Latrobe Valley Express*, www.latrobevalleyexpress.com.au)

(OAM), is a parochial and celebratory rendition of his migration journey that serves a mainstream political purpose. The choice of inscription below the statue speaks most explicitly to these sentiments – to the finality of migration to Australia, and to the successful project of mass immigration as a means to secure 'New Australians':

> 'The Migrant'
> A suitcase filled with courage,
> Wonder, hope and dreams

In search of far horizons
For what fate and fortune brings

I have found you land of freedom
No longer will I roam
My tomorrows are your destiny
Australia, my home
　　　　　A poem by D. Tripodi

Most immediately, the poem juts up against more recent political rhetoric that denies the offer of sanctuary to irregular migrants and asylum seekers, and indeed the much longer history of border control and denial of entry to racialised peoples. The earlier discussion about walls as symbols for the border also hinted at these paradoxes contained in the visual representations at the Park. The poem also perpetuates a colonial mentality: demonstrating the ways in which ethnicised communities have 'contributed to the idea of Australia as a home', drawing on versions of historical victim narratives, of persecution in their countries of origin, and ultimately stories of contributing to Australian society, to justify their intensively felt, if relatively recent, sense of belonging to stolen land.[174]

The migrant success story is a dehistrocised trope; it is an uncomplicated and linear version of the settlement trajectory. If we were to search for alternative meanings in this inscription, we could underline its first-person voice and its open-ended optimism to argue that it centres migrant subjectivity, but to what effect? This, and the use of stories like Don's, compels me to ask: How do we fight against the conservative revisionist co-opting of our migration histories? One tact might be to assertively claim belonging to the settler-colonial state, as the poem does, but this is not a progressive or ethically defensible stance. The objective is to complicate simplistic public narratives about migration as progress and national becoming, especially if we are to reconcile with our history of racial injustice and their ongoing legacies. Curthoys explained this in relation to the failure of multiculturalism: 'As long as multiculturalism continues to fail to recognise the continuing power and salience of colonialism, the latter will continue to exercise its power, and the former will remain an aspiration rather than a condition of life.'[175] The Victorian Multicultural Community Infrastructure Fund, for which Committee was successful in 2014, still participates in these silences. In particular, the Fund's reference to the 'Multicultural Policy Statement', underpinned by the 'Victorian Values Statement', makes no

---

[174] Ann Curthoys, 'An Uneasy Conversation: The Multicultural and the Indigenous', in *Race, Colour and Identity in Australia and New Zealand*, ed. John Docker and Gerhard Fischer (Sydney: University of New South Wales Press, 2000), 34.

[175] Ibid., 34.

mention of Indigenous Australia or the deep and ongoing violence of structural racism and its effects on ethnicised and racialised communities.[176]

As stated, the Committee was able to strategically draw on a celebratory state-endorsed liberalist multiculturalism to gain funding and support from government bodies, and the poem is a part of this rhetoric. My interest here extended to the 'gaps' created by such efforts, and the imaginative leaps and links we might make with other histories of immigration. For example, while Don participates in nationalist and revisionist framings of his past, subsumed as it is within a wider narrative of post-war success and progress, he also speaks of translocal and class-bound place making, his active efforts to find home and commonality in a multi-ethnic Gippsland. His diasporic sensibility saw him engaged in local soccer, local migrant-owned businesses, and ultimately the making of the Gippsland Immigration Park in Morwell. Don's own writings about his life offer a more complex image, in which migration is determined by both 'push' and 'pull' factors, tied to war and poverty, and in which we're able to gain insight into the wider structures influencing his migration and settlement, a narrative that is not linear or easily encapsulated by one trope.

Like many others, Don's migration trajectory was not without its own difficulties and years of substandard accommodation and dangerous work within Australia. Arrival was not the end point in this migration journey. Other migrants of his cohort experienced further and continual mobility within Australia under the terms of their two-year work contracts with the government, and beyond that period, as they followed the availability of work and accommodation for non-English speaking migrants in an assimilationist Australia. Don's story is not every man's story. But itinerant migrant workers are a key part of this history, their status as migrant and worker shaped their settlement journeys, which were anything but linear. The statue, therefore, can be read as a homage to mobility, a requiem to instability, and a reminder of the isolation of these experiences. It speaks to a specific historical subjectivity – the male working-class white European post-war migrant in regional Australia, a historical marker that works to undermine other celebratory elements of the Park. Perhaps it also speaks to the difficulty of finding 'belonging' on unceded Indigenous lands. In foregrounding the unsettled, uncertain status of 'the migrant', the statue undermines the linear and progressive narrative of settlement upon which the myth of harmonious multiculturalism relies. In this framing, the Park's statue adheres to a politics of recognition that rejects the surface level celebration of 'food and folklore' that has

---

[176] Victoria State Government, 'Multicultural Community Infrastructure Fund', 2019–2020, https://content.vic.gov.au/sites/default/files/2019-11/multicultural-community-infrastructure-fund-2019-2020-guidelines.pdf

typified multiculturalism in Australia, in favour of material and structural demands for heritage recognition.

3 Recognising Coal: De/Industrial Heritage and Migrant Workplaces in Community Narratives

A few popular narratives are associated with the Latrobe Valley. Not all of them work well together. The one I heard locals utter when I first visited in 2018 was 'coal is king', delivered with a sardonic and tired smile. This line is familiar to many long-time residents of the Latrobe Valley. While it may once have been earnestly delivered, it is now tempered by other perceptions of the Valley, namely that of government neglect and high unemployment.

The need to transition away from brown and black coal is a big part of this discussion. Australia's energy market is still dominated by coal, mostly black coal, but brown coal, for which the Latrobe Valley is known, is more polluting. The environmental aspects of the debate, however, are only one part of this public discussion. The contested, double-edged nature of coal mining in Australia's history also shapes perceptions. While coal may be king, its effects on community and public health, and the suffering it has wrought on individual workers, makes it contested terrain on which to sustain a community identity. This, combined with more recent community memories of privatisation, government neglect, and high unemployment in the Valley, shapes community attachments and associations with industrial heritage.

Using the Park's storyboard plaques as starting points, this section will explore community debates around the remains of industry, alongside a history of workplaces, safety, and public health, especially as they were experienced and remembered by migrant workers. The storyboard plaques on the walls of the Park depict these structures as well as the migrant men who worked in them. The plaques do important heritage work. They centre migrant bodies in the workplace and push for a recognition of working-class history; they also recognise this working-class history as one defined by difference and being migrant. I draw on these depictions to tell a particular history: to stress the centrality of migrant peoples in popularly revered narratives around coal. Due to the contested nature of these narratives, and associated community debates about industrial heritage, these representations of difference and migrant working life can also be read as subaltern, contradictory, and even subversive acts of recognition in a landscape shaped by many silences.

In drawing attention to difference, in challenging the Anglo-centrism of coal mining narratives, in their undeniable connections to workplaces and the damage they can inflict, the storyboard plaques adhere to a politics of recognition. The aim for 'parity of representation' is a key part of this politics.[177] Section 2's reading of the statue argued that as mobile members of families constrained by material conditions, male migrant subjects asserted (and continue to assert) their need for recognition and representation. The Park and its commemorative components are a platform for that assertion, which operate at the local (Morwell), regional (the Latrobe Valley), and national level (Australia). The history of migrant subjects in the region, in industry, and in working life is presented as a pathway to recognition: highlighting the paucity of non-Anglo representation in official heritage, the history of structural differences within the workplace that affected migrant lives, and, following on from this, the need for material redistribution.

Forms of marginalisation or privilege intersect along multiple axes of oppression. These sets of social relations create inequalities that are perpetuated through the flows of labour and capital across places like the Latrobe Valley, which in turn give meaning to those landscapes. The symbolic and the structural are difficult to separate here. For example, stereotypes of work in the Latrobe Valley are culturally masculinised, and the public sphere is dominated by Anglo-Australian perspectives on history. This also relates to privilege and power held in workforces, community politics, and, of course, heritage practices and discourses.

I focus on the Park's presentation of non-Anglo-Australian working life and the labouring individuals and families behind the facades of industry – most notably coal mining and power stations – as a means to tell alternative histories. These histories can offer a 'radical nostalgia'. As argued throughout this Element, this nostalgia is not a lament for a bygone, contained, and safe world; nor is it a romanticisation of the 'diversity' of past workplaces (the latter in line with revisionist multicultural discourses now attached to the postwar era – for example, descriptions of the National Heritage Listed site of Bonegilla Migrant Camp as a 'Little Europe' and a 'birthplace of multiculturalism').[178] Nostalgia has been an important aspect of the radical imagination over time and need not be understood solely as reactionary.[179] Rather, and as the previous section demonstrated, the Park's nostalgia relies on centring the migrant subject and drawing attention to the historic and structural circumstances under which they laboured. This nostalgia, therefore, aspires to a reality based on economic redistribution and cultural recognition.

---

[177] Nancy Fraser, 'Social Justice in the Knowledge Society: Redistribution, Recognition, and Participation', *Heinrich Boll Stiftung* 5 (2001): 27.

[178] See Dellios, *Histories of Controversy*; Ashton, 'The Birthplace of Australian Multiculturalism'.

[179] Bonnett, *Left in the Past*.

The Park is here read as documenting the experience of the past to inform more just and inclusive futures.

As in Section 2, subsections in this section aim to demonstrate the role of ethnic and class difference in shaping workplace experiences in the Valley, and thus the compelling heritage work the Park can do in drawing attention to structural discrimination. At the same time, I am weary of suggesting that the Park represents the migrant subject as economic agent only, without an identity beyond the SECV machine or coal mining. In the case of the Park, migrant subjects are asserting their history in the region, in industry and working life, and in cultural life. These representations of migrant subjects are defined by more than just their ethnic contributions to a white managerial multicultural nation state.

Collective struggles to remember or forget the industrial heritage of the region are encompassed by a key community narrative: that of state care and neglect. The narrative relates to privatisation and high unemployment from the 1990s, neglectful practices around hazard reduction at power plants and public health issues in subsequent decades, as well as earlier unsafe workplace experiences. Some community associations with the SECV and its promise of 'jobs for life' are romanticised; however, people have expressed plenty of stories about unsafe workplaces and memories of strike action. These contested memories are inscribed on the commemorative forms of the Park. Furthermore, while local histories of the towns in the Valley celebrate the coal industry, they are unable to avoid a key fact: planning and development restrictions inhibit towns like Morwell by privileging the extraction of brown coal deposits above community well-being and environmental security.[180] People have felt pushed aside by the interests of industry and large mining companies. Community heritage concerns rank lowest, an issue that is not limited to the industrial heritage in the Latrobe Valley.[181] As Denis Byrne argues, 'catastrophic events may be "buried" by the state's control of official history but this does not mean they cannot be recuperated by local action'.[182] The Park does this work of recuperation; it is heritage as social action. The Gippsland Immigration Park is unavoidably bound up in discussions and public history narratives around: working life and conditions for migrant workers at the SECV, the individual and community effects of privatisation from the 1990s, the devastating mine fire of 2014, and the function

---

[180] Latrobe City Council, 'Latrobe Planning Scheme Planning Scheme Review Report', April 2008, www.latrobe.vic.gov.au/sites/default/files/Latrobe_Planning_Scheme_Review_Report_April_2008.pdf

[181] Peter Spearritt, 'Money, Taste and Industrial Heritage', *Australian Historical Studies* 24, no. 96 (1991): 33–45.

[182] Byrne, 'A Critique of Unfeeling Heritage', 234.

and ethics of preserving industrial heritage in the midst of climate disaster and long-term health concerns.

Reading Industrial and Labour Heritage

Historian Peter Spearritt noted in the 1990s that industrial heritage was little appreciated by heritage 'professionals' and the public. Labour history was booming in Australia, but historians had little input into the heritage space, leaving the listing and conservation of industrial heritage structures and places to architects.[183] 'Money and taste', Spearritt argued, determined the conservation of industrial heritage, rather than historical or cultural significance.[184] A more 'values-based management' ethos has since suffused the heritage management sector in Australia; however, as heritage scholars Smith, Schakel, and Campbell noted, when sites of labour are presented on Australian heritage lists and registers, the stories of working-class people themselves are rarely featured. The sites are instead celebrated for technical or industrial innovations and have little to say about the people whose labour underwrote those industries. With this in mind, historians Reeves et al. drew a clear distinction between 'industrial' and 'labor' heritage: 'If industrial history concerns itself with technologies, with sites of work and workforce development, labour history is above all concerned with the people who worked the machines, populated the factories, mines and mills or depended on them for their livelihood.'[185] But as they and heritage practitioners like Chris Johnston also argue, 'heritage without history' – industrial heritage without historical grounding, without an analysis of the lives bound up in these physical sites – can only serve to produce a 'static profile of a lost past'.[186] Collective memories of coal mining, in particular, are contested emotional terrain. Representations must contend with the 'dignity' attached to early mining work and the key role mining played in colonisation and the consolidation of the Australian nation state, but also with the history of industrial relations, and the radical insurgency of miners and Australian unionism.[187] Mining therefore holds an ambiguous position in the history and imagination of the Left.

In some cases, my approach to the Park requires some reading against the grain. For one, the links between power, industry, and identity are obvious if we consult the listed donors to the Park. The Committee received some funding from power companies and other large industries, including Australian Paper

---

[183] Spearritt, 'Money, Taste and Industrial Heritage', 34–35.
[184] See also Johnston and Australian Heritage Commission, *What Is Social Value?*
[185] Reeves et al., 'Broken Hill', 313.   [186] Ibid.
[187] See Ibid.; and Erik Eklund, *Mining Towns: Making a Living, Making a Life* (Sydney: University of New South Wales Press, 2012).

Maryvale, Loy Lang Power, International Power Hazelwood, International Power Loy Lang B, and TRU Energy. Reading the plaque's depiction of the Latrobe Valley's power stations as an advert, or even a retrograde nostalgia for a 'golden era' of coal, would be easy. Nevertheless, migrant families, social clubs, and local small business also contributed, and the 'bit of a story' that the Committee aspired to create through these plaques can do much more besides tracking industrial progress.[188] There are many parts to this whole; this heritage is complex and multi-storied, and instances of recognition and misrecognition play out as specific practices of heritage making at the Park.

Plaques: 'The Immigration Story'

The Park's storyboard plaques directly engage with both the celebration and contestation of the region's coal industry heritage, and the workers who both benefitted from and were damaged by their work. These parts of the Park provide a platform for a radical nostalgia that reimagines the migrant subject in the history of the coal industry – one that centres working lives, in addition to material and economic realities. The Park's narratives around the coal industry in the Latrobe Valley, and migrant workers' mobility, have the potential to do radical heritage work, even as it participates in the broader settler-colonial project to erase the sovereignty of First Nations' people.

In total, twelve storyboard plaques appear across three granite walls. The Committee chose to begin the 'Immigration Story' of Gippsland ('From the World to Gippsland') with depictions of transportation – ships and planes – alongside maps of the world, Australia, and Gippsland. Here, the Committee begins the migrant story with the invasion of Australia by Europeans. On one level, casting all settlers as migrants could be approached as a radical reimagining of conventional Anglo-centric histories of the nation. Such histories traditionally cast Anglo-Celtic arrivals (especially pre-WWII) as 'pioneers' who 'settled' the land, distinct from those ethnicised post–WWII migrants who maintain a marginal status in relation to the white-settler mainstream and whose 'belonging' always remains under scrutiny. However, casting all arrivals since 1788 as migrants also collapses the motivations of respective waves of immigration, the push and pull factors of mobility, and the changing racial and class constraints facing new arrivals to Australia. It ignores, most importantly, the difficult matter of 'belonging' on someone else's country.

Alternatively, I could argue that the Park's plaques do not look backward and imagine a pre- and post-diverse Australia; rather, they imagine the presence of 'Others' in Australia as a constant in the continent's post-invasion history. The

---

[188] Di Fabrizio, 'Author's Interview with the Committee'.

Figure 12 Wall one of the Gippsland Immigration Park (photo taken by the author)

Park's 2007 *Souvenir Booklet* picks out nationalities – the Swiss, the Danish, the French-Canadians, the Germans, and the Chinese – as part of a 'great cosmopolitan mix' that expanded across the Gippsland region from 1840. But while attention is paid to the relationship with the landscape – to gold mining, dairy

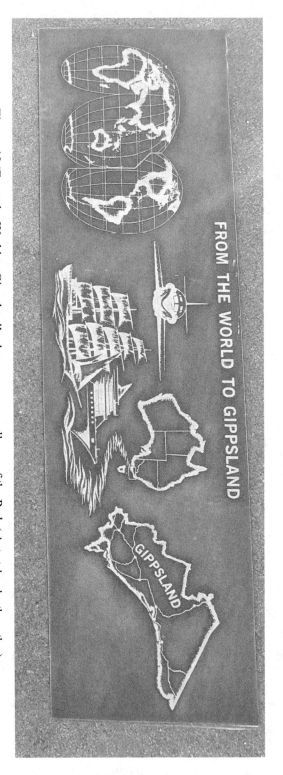

Figure 13 'From the World to Gippsland': plaque one on wall one of the Park (photo taken by the author)

farms and brown coal – the effect is to also erase a deeper relationship to country and to the land's original inhabitants, the Gunai Kurnai, and thus to ignore questions around the migrant's responsibility to First Nation's people and to knowing the history of the lands on which they settle. 'We're all migrants here' therefore does little to unpack a settler-colonial mentality. The second plaque, 'Migration into Gippsland' – depicting three European male explorers, Angus McMillan, Paul Strzelecki, and Alfred William Hewitt, which was addressed in the previous section – participates more explicitly in this whitewashing of Australia's settler history, positioning the expansion of the settler-colonial project as benign migration, rather than the expulsion of Traditional Custodians.

Plaque three, 'Departing & Arriving', contains those depictions of migration with which we have become familiar since the twentieth century: the passport, groups of people on board the passenger liner, the dock filled with people either farewelling loved ones or welcoming new arrivals, and the post-war migrant camp. A ship appears on this plaque four times – M/S Anna Salen, M/S Australia at the Port of Genoa, and another two ships dockside – reflecting the ship's iconic place in the story of post-war mass migration to Australia. The imagery on this plaque references the experiences of migrants arriving from 1949 to the 1960s mostly from the British Isles and continental Europe. 'Arriving' extends to travel to Gippsland from Melbourne, and arrival at the migrant camp: in this case, West Sale Migrant Camp, run by the Department of Immigration, and located in South-East Gippsland. Many of these photos are sourced from private family collections, and therefore reference family histories of arrival.[189] Such photographs play a key role in documenting not only changing relationships to the industrial landscape, but also changing types of work and workers in the Valley. Presented here, they are stimulus for public discussions about changing land use, workplaces and workplace practices and technologies, and wider shifts in cultural attitudes to these stereotypes around the 'worker' in heavy industry.

Plaque four depicts all the major power stations in the Latrobe Valley; plaques five to eight (on wall two) depict aspects of 'Working Life', and plaques nine to twelve (on wall three) depict 'Settling In', which is dedicated to community sporting and cultural clubs (most obviously, Don's Morwell Falcons, described in Section 2). The focus for the remainder of this section will be plaques four to eight: the power stations and working life.

---

[189] The description for one of the bus images reads: 'The Boeren family came to Gippsland from Holland in 1955. They travelled by bus from Melbourne. Here they have stopped for a break and taken a photo of the family in front of the bus.' Gippsland Immigration Park Committee, 'Gippsland Immigration Wall of Recognition'.

The 'Golden Era' of the SECV

The names of the power stations and major industrial sites are contained on plaque four: Yallourn power station, Morwell power station and briquette factory, Hazelwood power station, Loy Yang A and B power stations, coal mining (collapsing all open-cut brown coal mines into one site depiction), and the Australian Paper Manufacturers' mill. Laying out all power stations, factories, and mines like this captures a sense of the Valley's dramatic industrial landscape. It also stands as a testament to the dramatic transformation of that landscape from its coal-powered past. Plaque four is about the material past: the sites that dominated the lives and fortunes of many residents of the Valley, including all members of the Committee.

Section 2 summarised the rapid growth of the SECV in the Valley, and especially Morwell, from the 1950s. In that decade, the SECV erected a new power station building, two briquette factory buildings, a coal bunker, a coal conveyer system, and accessory buildings.[190] Community narratives reference the 'slow, easy, comfortable' work available at the SECV from the fifties to the seventies.[191] Journalist Tom Doig, in his exploration of the 2014 Hazelwood mine fire, references those earlier times, when 'thousands of men had "jobs for life"; brothers, cousins, in-laws and sons could all get work at one of the Valley's huge mines or power stations'.[192] Such narratives, and the pride associated with mine work, are often attached to this bygone era. However, in many grassroots tellings, the SECV are hardly always the 'good guys'. Doig goes on to summarise the ambivalent situation facing SECV workers thus: 'wages and life expectancy rates weren't great, but job security and community spirit were unparalleled'.[193] Memories of protracted union disputes, of SECV zoning restrictions, and unfair compensation are widespread in the Valley. These histories are a key part of the wider story of industry and labour in the region, in Australia, and other industrialised nations. Grievances about the SECV (and by proxy the state) prioritising coal above community are perhaps a truer origin for the phrase 'coal is king'.

Nostalgia and Deindustrialised Working-Class Communities

Undeniably, the romanticism associated with the coal mining past is a largely Anglo-Australian vision, which obscures the culturally diverse reality of that past. The symbolic value attached to older working-class identities associated with the era of mass employment in heavy industry, mining, and construction – those

---

[190] Legg, *Heart of the Valley*, 232.   [191] Doig, *Hazelwood*, 60–67.   [192] Ibid., 67.
[193] Ibid., 68.

Figure 14 Major projects, plaque four on wall one (photo taken by the author)

identities now depicted as 'directionless and abject in the aftermath of industrial closure and joblessness' – is overwhelmingly white.[194]

The Park's storyboard plaques stand as a challenge to the widespread exclusion of migrant and refugee peoples from public platforms; furthermore, they stress civic responsibilities alongside a need for equitable public services, effectively rerouting the reactionary impulse of the nostalgia often associated with pride in industry. The Park's website describes some of the themes presented in the text and images: 'Life in Gippsland, Government, Rule of Law, Transport, Educating Gippsland, Serving Gippsland (emergency services) and Gippsland Community (immigrants, early sport, population, government towns).' All the imagery on the plaques are of groups of workers, they are relational, and they are shown working as part of teams, whether that be in the industrial workplace, or in civic and cultural life. As a whole, they may be read as a celebration of communitarian ethics, made especially pertinent in a deindustrialised, neoliberal, and increasingly individualised workplace. As the structures and people depicted on the plaques demonstrate, this communitarian ethics, even in a forgotten and deindustrialising regional centre, is something that requires active effort, a working aspiration for the future.

All of this is to say that nostalgia can be deployed in different ways. In Section 1, I referenced a new body of literature that has a more sophisticated approach to the emotion of nostalgia.[195] Smith and Campbell, for example, treat nostalgia as being 'sincere, authentic, enabling, present and future centred and capable of positively addressing trauma'.[196] The memory work being performed at the Park is capable of addressing many of the complex and potentially traumatic memories of industrial work in the Latrobe Valley, while also looking fondly back on an era of relatively secure employment and community participation. The material representation of this labouring past is important, especially for the migrant subjects implicated in its retelling. The structures of industry depicted on plaque four are therefore emotional anchors: for, as Byrne and others have argued through their research, 'most people in the world relate to the material past via their emotions'.[197]

Don Di Fabrizio's personal past is deeply implicated in this material, as the discussion on the statue in Section 2 demonstrated. He spoke to me about helping build that industrial landscape. His company DIFABRO was contracted to erect steel for parts of Hazelwood power station, also depicted in plaque four. During the course of our interview in 2019, he was able to point out his kitchen window to Hazelwood, a structure he helped build, a tangible marker of his migrant presence in the landscape. The eight chimneys of Hazelwood were demolished in May 2020,

---

[194] Dicks, 'Performing the Hidden Injuries of Class in Coal-Mining Heritage', 437.

[195] Smith and Campbell, 'Nostalgia for the future', 612. [196] Ibid.

[197] Byrne, 'A Critique of Unfeeling Heritage', 249.

with the remainder of the station to follow. Don never expressed to me a desire to have the structure conserved, codified, and listed on an official heritage register. Perhaps his efforts through the Park have fulfilled these emotional needs to retain a record of the industrial and working lives of migrants in the region. These efforts run parallel and separate from the AHD that governs lists and registers.

Working Life and Traumatic Memories of Industry

Plaques five to eight depict 'Working Life'. Plaque five depicts the 'original' primary industries of the Latrobe Valley and the West Gippsland region, forestry and dairy farming, especially around the towns of Drouin, Warragul, and Narracan. Alternatively, plaques six and seven are exclusively focused on the construction and power industries. Unlike plaque four's depiction of power stations in the Valley, they depict people at work, rather than only the structures and landscapes of the power industry. Plaque six, in an effort to extend the scope of the Park to all of Gippsland (rather than just the Latrobe Valley), references the history of shipping in Gippsland. Shipping is depicted along the coastline, the lakes and rivers, showing migrants at work in boat yards, as well as mine workers from earlier coal mines at Wonthaggi, Coalville, and Kilcunda in the period from the 1870s to the 1940s.

Figure 15 Plaque five and six on wall two; Farming and Timber, early mining and shipping (photo taken by the author)

Plaque seven also shows men at work. It depicts a group of post-war migrant men working alongside powerlines and trucks loaded with pre-fabricated steel for the Loy Yang power station in 1985; migrant men working with concrete foundations for the Morwell power station in 1953; the three brothers Di Fabrizio consulting planning works in their Morwell workshop office in 1978; workers from DIFABRO erecting steel at Hazelwood power station in 1962; a maintenance crew at the SEC Yallourn Centre workshops in 1964, and another group of migrant workers at the Loy Yang power station in 1982. Many of the photos used for plaque seven come from the Di Fabrizio Collection, showing workers from their steel fabrication plants. Most men are turned away from the camera, leaning over workbenches or looking up at large industrial structures in their hard hats. A few look directly at the camera, a couple with a smile and at least one on his smoke break.

Like plaque four, plaque seven aims to showcase the 'importance of the power industry to the development of Gippsland and where so many immigrants worked'.[198] All of the workers shown in plaques five to seven are men of mostly continental European origin. The issue of women's low employment in the Latrobe Valley is long-standing, and the Park does little to alleviate their civic invisibility, but it also reflects the male-centred vision of the Valley and the government's approach to supporting employment in the region. Recent socio-logical studies of Gippsland and its employment policies reveal a deeply ingrained valorisation of 'masculinised employment' in the region.[199] Men and masculinised industries are understood as the norm, even if the Latrobe Valley's workforce is now typified by those who work in allied health services and community service provision, areas traditionally dominated by women. Farhall, Tyler, and Fairbrother found that recently published regional planning documents are part of the problem. They perpetuate gendered forms of social organisation by marginalising the role and status of women in the Gippsland workforce.

Plaque eight, the final in the 'Working Life' series, depicts men and women in small business and secondary industries: the Auciello family's soft drink factory Alpine Beverages in Morwell (established in 1947), family-run salons, the Morwell La Mode clothing factory that employed local migrant women, the work of a stonemason, shoe repairer and painter, and workers at West Sale migrant camp. The lack of employment opportunities for women during the Valley's Golden Age was a big social concern, and the reason

[198] Gippsland Immigration Park Committee, 'Gippsland Immigration Wall of Recognition'.
[199] Kate Farhall, Meagan Tyler, and Peter Fairbrother, 'Labour and Regional Transition: Sex-Segregation, the Absence of Gender and the Valorisation of Masculinised Employment in Gippsland, Australia', *Gender, Place & Culture* 28, no. 12 (2021), 1755–1777

Figure 16 Plaque seven and eight on wall two. Working in power stations/men on site, working in secondary industries and small business (photo taken by the author)

behind the push for 'secondary developments', like the two factories erected at Morwell (1945) and Traralgon (1951) by La Mode. These factories produced undergarments and employed about 400 women. They closed in 1965 when the company encountered financial difficulties due to a credit squeeze. Despite its short life, memories of work and working life at these factories left a community impression. Plaque eight depicts six women working on the assembly line at La Mode; they are paused in their work and staring directly into the camera.

The plaques contain a remarkable amount of detail. Most of the images come from family collections, rather than state records offices or the archives of big industry. At first glance, they are celebratory and positive depictions of working life in Gippsland and the Latrobe Valley. They participate in the glorification of the power industry and its central role in the development of the region. However, they also offer intimate portraits, and compel us to look closer at actual working people and working lives. Hinting perhaps at those flashpoints in the Valley's traumatic history of heavy industry, the men depicted here are dwarfed by large industrial structures: concrete drainage pipes, large overhead power lines, steel mills, and blast furnaces. This was specialised, dangerous, and often dirty work. And for migrant workers, their experiences of the industrial workplace were shaped by ethnic discrimination. Looking at a broader canvas, Armstrong argued in the 1990s that migrant heritage places relating to industrial work were 'places of great humiliation', in which they faced boundaries to promotion and equitable treatment.[200] These are recent memories for many post-war migrants, including those depicted in the Park's plaques. Beyond the traumatic, however, these incidences also demonstrate a history of migrant workers' pursuit of improved working conditions and collective rights – stories which, as labour historian Lucy Taksa has also argued, have not been a feature of either museum depictions of immigration or industrial heritage in Australia.[201]

The 1977 SECV Strike

In late 1977, approximately 2,500 maintenance workers employed by the SECV went on strike for 11 weeks. The Victorian branch of the left-wing Amalgamated Metal Workers and Shipwrights' Union (AMWSU) released a pamphlet in 1978 on the events. This was an early attempt to document the history of that strike and inscribe it into the 'proud tradition of militant trade unionism' in Australia.[202] The AMWSU's pamphlet also captured, in dramatic fashion, the ambivalence of workers to industry and life in the Valley:

> [R]ich pasture and rolling hills stand in stark contrast to the raw, brown open-cut mines that sear its surface, and to the giant coolers and smoke stacks that dominate the skyline. Equally, the apparent calm, peace and tranquillity of the people of the Valley masks a seething and bitter discontent, an inflamed sense of injustice that exists like the brown coal in the area. And like brown coal, it's very near the surface.[203]

The emotive language here – workers' 'seething and bitter discontent' – gives new meaning to Doig's later historical assessment of poor wages and life expectancy, despite 'job security and community spirit'.[204] The existence of this community spirit was evidently precarious, much like the precarity of dwellings resting on coal-bearing land in Morwell. The prioritising of coal

---

[200] Helen Armstrong, 'Mapping Migrant Memories: Crossing Cultural Borders', *Journal of the Oral History Association of Australia*, no. 19 (1997): 59–65.

[201] Lucy Taksa, 'Labor History and Public History in Australia: Allies or Uneasy Bedfellows?' *International Labor and Working-Class History*, no. 76 (2009): 84–85.

[202] Amalgamated Metal Workers and Shipwrights' Union (AMWSU) (Australia), Victorian State Branch, *The 1977 Latrobe Valley Power Strike* (East Melbourne: Amalgamated Metal Workers and Shipwrights' Union, Victorian State Branch, 1978).

[203] Ibid.   [204] Doig, *Hazelwood,* 68.

and profits, above workers' lives, was made apparent in events like the 1977 strike.

The strike had far-reaching and immediate effects on all the people of Victoria: severe power restrictions were imposed across the state. Almost 500,000 workers were temporarily stood down, and the state government amended the Essential Services Act 1958 (Vic) to declare a state of emergency. Union histories note the 'uncompromising hostility' displayed by the SECV and the state government towards employees, the Union, and the coordinating body the Central Gippsland Trades and Labour Council (CGTLC).[205] Kathryn May Steel's PhD research indicates that the response of the SECV over the key pressure point of contract labour made the whole affair especially emotive. As discussed, the myth around the SECV offering secure 'jobs for life' was and is a widespread one in the Valley, but the low wages (Latrobe Valley power workers were paid less than their counterparts in other states, especially the trade assistants) and the use of contract labour was a long-standing area of disagreement between maintenance workers and the SECV. The latter was seen to be scaling back its permanent workforce and drawing on private contractors rather than permanent SECV staff to perform maintenance works.

Maintenance workers logged a series of grievances and demands with the SECV in March 1977, including calls for a new special award and bans on contracted work. They received no adequate response from the company. Putting the matter before the Australian Conciliation and Arbitration Commission (ACAC) led to more disappointment for workers. The SECV gave notice that it would appeal any arbitration decision that granted the workers' claims. In any case, their claims for a wage increase were rejected by ACAC, after which the workers called for a strike.

John Halfpenny, State (Victoria) Secretary of the AMWSU, who presented the ACAC decision to workers, implicated government interference, as did subsequent CGTLC publications. Their words demonstrate the ongoing influence of Cold War politics on industrial disputes in Australia: 'the Commonwealth Government was busy bashing "communists" and "pommy shop stewards", while [Prime Minister] Fraser sought a means of denying to hundreds of thousands of stood down workers in a bid to impose further pressure on the maintenance workers in the Valley'.[206] John Halfpenny was a member of the Communist Party of Australia at the time of the dispute. His colleague, Sam Armstrong – a Scottish immigrant, a shop steward for the AMWSU, secretary of their Latrobe Valley branch, and President of the CGTLC from 1975 to 1985 – also had affiliations with the party. Another key

---

[205] AMWSU, *The 1977 Latrobe Valley Power Strike.*   [206] Ibid.

figure, George Wragg – an English migrant, and at the time of the dispute, a shop steward for the AMWSU, President of the Latrobe Valley Branch of the AMWSU, Executive Committee member of the CGTLC, and a member of the CGTLC Disputes Committee – had been involved in the reorganisation of the CGTLC in the 1960s, wrestling power away from the conservative, anti-Communist, and Catholic forces in 1960. Accounts of the 1977 strike cast these three men, and a few others with decades of experience in the trade union movement, as the leaders in the dispute with the SECV. Aside from Wragg and Armstrong, who were migrants from the British Isles, I've found no records of migrant workers involved in the high-level negotiations between the unions and the SECV, despite non-British migrants constituting the largest proportion of the SECV workforce. Unlike most rural background migrants from Southern Europe, and some Eastern European migrants suspicious of organised labour, migrants from industrial hubs in the British Isles arrived in Australia with a familiar experience of unionism. British migrants were able to assimilate themselves into existing Anglo-Australia trade union practices and hierarchies to gain leadership roles.

Despite the diverse politics of this migrant cohort, after decades of mass migration from mainly continental Europe and the British Isles, the Valley workforce in the 1960s held a reputation for collective strength and union militancy. The migrant-dominated SECV workforce was almost completely unionised.[207] However, as June Hearn argued in the 1970s, those from non-Anglo-Australian backgrounds were underrepresented in fulltime union positions.[208] In the immediate post-war years, only the far left and militant unions with ties to the Communist Party of Australia (CPA), who explicitly opposed the White Australia Policy, made efforts to engage the non-British migrant workforce. And even then, they did not come close to parity of representation in positions of leadership. Non-Anglophone migrant demands that union hierarchies change and more seriously consider the needs of their non-English-speaking members reached a fever-pitch in the 1970s, especially with the 1973 Migrant Workers' Conference held in Melbourne. Papers emerging from this conference reveal a fuller picture of migrant political engagement in the workplace than materials around the 1977 SECV strike.[209]

---

[207] Kathryn M. Steel, 'Point of View: A Significant Regional Industrial Dispute from a Novel Perspective', *Provenance: The Journal of Public Record Office Victoria*, no. 12 (2013).

[208] June Hearn, *Migrant Experiences in Trade Unions: A Study of Migrant Participation in Leadership in Victorian Trade Unions*, PhD thesis, University of Melbourne, 1974.

[209] Papers from the Migrant Workers' Conference (Melbourne 7–9 October 1973) printed in Des Storer and Centre for Urban Research & Action, eds., *Ethnic Rights, Power and Participation Toward a Multi-Cultural Australia* (Melbourne: Clearing House on Migration Issues, Ecumenical Migration Centre and Centre for Urban Research and Action, 1975).

Socialist groups recounting the 1977 strike argue that it could have been won if the unions had fully mobilised the rank and file, the shop-floor organisation. Trade union officials missed an opportunity to use their rank-and-file network to build support from the wider community.[210] Current members of the Greek Elderly Citizens Club in Morwell recall those tough weeks of the 1977 strike but had no comment on the higher-level negotiations that occurred, aside from a vaguely articulated sense of betrayal. Ultimately, the strike and its disappointing end resulted in few wins for the workers. Disputes between the CGTLC and SECV over the use of contract labour continued throughout the 1970s and 1980s, and up until the company's privatisation.

Although most the workers depicted in plaques six and seven of the Park are workers for the SECV, or construction workers working at SECV sites (like DIFABRO employees), we need not read these depictions as a glorification of SECV. Rather, the focus is on people at work, and not only the products of their labour. As I hope I've demonstrated, that narrative can never be one of simple celebration: the community's relationship to the SECV was and is complicated and contested. The 1977 strike is just one example of that. Working in heavy industry was not all happiness and prosperity. The damaging aspects of industry are harder to represent in a monument or statue. The details contained in the storyboard plaques, therefore, are especially important to the Park's overall heritage work, and the work of political recognition. While the region was relatively unscathed by global oil crises in the 1970s, the period was typified by heightened industrial action on the part of several unions.[211] Many of the names that appear on the Wall of Recognition are of those who participated in these strikes, and campaigned for migrant and workers' rights throughout the 1960s and 1970s. Hard-earned fights over migrant workers' rights, migrant rights to citizenship, and union representation occurred in tandem with rising concerns over the environmental impact of the coal industry and toxic industrial waste in the Valley.[212] Growth was associated with development; change was progress. However, as local historian Legg conceded, this outlook could not be maintained when quality of life issues forced a re-interpretation of the region's past and future.[213]

---

[210] Solidarity, 'Latrobe Valley 1977 Power Strike', 8 September 2017, www.solidarity.net.au /unions/latrobe-valleys-1977-power-strike/

[211] The Gippsland Institute of Advanced Education to the Town and Country Planning Board, State Electricity Commission of Victoria, Country Roads Board, and Central Gippsland Social Survey, *A Socio-Economic Study of the Latrobe Valley: A Report* (Melbourne: C. H. Rixon, Government Printer, 1975).

[212] Legg, *Heart of the Valley*, 298.   [213] Ibid., 280–299.

Migrant Workers and Vulnerability

Workplace accidents are another obvious place to start when searching for alternative pasts associated with the Valley's coal industry. Some of the migrant community testimony linked to the Gippsland Immigration Park references these histories. The 2012 booklet *Stories from the Gippsland Immigration Wall of Recognition* featured written testimony from people inscribed on the Park's Wall of Recognition and depicted on the storyboard plaques. 'A Tragic Start in a New Country' recounts the story of Bernard Aalbers, who migrated on assisted passage from the Netherlands in 1957. Less than a year later, '[w]hile working near the briquette factory [in Morwell] he was killed and on the 5th birthday of his youngest child, Maria, he was buried'.[214] The sense of loss and calamity this workplace accident inflicted on the newly arrived Dutch family was felt across generations. It shaped their immediate fortunes, and their long-term orientations to heavy industry in the region. The Aalbers' family relied on support from the local Dutch community in Morwell, as Mrs Aalbers spent years negotiating workers compensation from the SECV. Despite this traumatic experience, the family wished to participate in the Park's commemorative work and include themselves in this monument that centres the power industry.

Migrant welfare groups and migrant rights activists made an issue of the lack of interpreters and translation in the workplace. Even left-wing trade unions, although eager to boost membership, were charged with negligence when it came to communicating workplace safety measures and workers' rights with migrants who spoke languages other than English.[215] Safety within the workplace is linked to this issue of communication. For migrant rights' activists like George Zangalis, who worked at General Motors Holden the 1950s and later as a Railway Unions representative, on-the-job English language lessons became a matter of safety: 'Employers were at first not happy – but [it produced] better outcomes, safety, educated workers.'[216] Records of workplace accidents and even deaths are difficult to trace, particularly with a large and now dissolved state-funded company like the SECV. Anecdotes abound within certain migrant communities, however. Eklund has argued that deaths through workplace incidents are a key but publicly absent theme in the history of the Valley, and that

214 Bernard and Coby Aalbers, *Stories from the Gippsland Immigration Wall of Recognition*, 6.
215 See Con George and George Zangalis' chapters in Storer and Centre for Urban Research & Action, *Ethnic Rights, Power and Participation Toward a Multi-Cultural Australia*.
216 George Zangalis interviewed by Kristina Kukolja in the Unwanted Australians oral history project – ORAL TRC 6920/1, National Library of Australia.

rates remain high, but these stories do not appear in museums or public sites relating to the industrial past.[217]

The Aalbers story is not unique across this period, or in any history of heavy industry. Such stories highlight the vulnerability of non-British migrant workers in Australia. Workplace accidents are one part of this history, and it relates to their employment insecurity and transience. While there was ample work available in the construction of power stations in the Latrobe Valley throughout the 1950s and 1960s, migrant workers were often the first to suffer during periods of economic downturn. For example, during the 'mini recession' of 1952, Morwell power station halted construction and all migrants who were not naturalised were the first to lose their jobs. Workplace discrimination against migrant workers was rife. From May 1952, social workers in the Department of Immigration reported on an increase in unemployed migrants seeking their help, most of whom were 'still under contract' and still living in migration centres. These migrants were victims of the 'last to come first to go' principle.[218] It's no surprise, then, that migrant workers supported the call to strike in 1977, and felt especially betrayed by union hierarchies when nothing came of their scarifies. Nonetheless, the collective memories of those eleven weeks, expressed by groups like the current Elderly Greek Citizens group, stress workers' solidarity above failure; they attach pride to their willingness to take their demands to the SECV and hold fast to collective action.

Asbestos, Air Pollution, and Workplace Health and Safety

In the 1970s, local groups continued to bemoan the creation of an industrial wasteland 'as gloomy as West Germany's Ruhr Valley'.[219] Constant grime and soot pervaded industrial settlements like the Latrobe Valley, as did the cantankerous noise and the smell of noxious effluent. However, even those who came to recognise the environmental impacts of industry sought to maintain a sense of optimism for the region's industrial future. In 1970, retired construction

---

[217] Erik Eklund, 'The Agents of Industrial Heritage in the Midst of Structural Transformation of the Latrobe Valley, Australia', in *Constructing Industrial Pasts: Heritage, Historical Culture and Identity in Regions Undergoing Structural Economic Transformation*, ed. Stefan Berger (Oxford, New York: Berghahn Books, 2020), 152.

[218] NAA, A445, 276/2/4, 'Unemployed Migrants: Confidential Report', Hazel Dobson to the Secretary for the Department of Immigration, 14 May 1952.

[219] *Fuel for Unrest: People, Power and Planning in the Latrobe Valley* (Melbourne: Brown Coal Study Group, Conservation Council of Victoria, 1981). Ironically, the Ruhr is now held up as a shining example of the 'successful mastering of de-industrialisation … arguably also the precondition for the valorisation of industrial heritage in the region', Berger and Pickering, 'Regions of Heavy Industry and Their Heritage–Between Identity Politics and 'Touristification': Where to Next? 1', in *Industrial Heritage and Regional Identities*, pp. 214–235 (Routledge, 2018).

engineer and local memoirist Cliff Wolfe wrote: 'Pollution of air and water will have its effect on the future of the Latrobe Valley, destined to become one of the great industrial centres of the Commonwealth.'[220] The rhetoric at this time was concerned with pollution and 'trade waste' – the disposal of waste from industry, especially from the Australian Paper Manufacturers' mill, and the pollution of the Latrobe River – rather than the broader climatic effects of burning fossil fuels. In the late 1960s, local papers reported on pollution in the Thomson, Latrobe, McAlister, and Mitchell Rivers, which flow into Gippsland Lakes, noting increased volumes of 'effluent and weed growth'.[221] However, despite the real impacts of the coal industry on community standards of living, and consistent community concerns about air quality, coal remained at the centre of many local people's vision for the future of the Latrobe Valley. The 'great activity' around construction and the expansion of the SECV during this era is captured most clearly in the images of work on the storyboard plaques.[222]

While Wolfe was unable to imagine a Valley without coal, he provided non-expert observations about the daily effects of the industry on community life, offering his own alarming and prophetic warnings:

> There are still times when vision is obscured by smog and this is accompanied by an unpleasant odour. This can easily be proved by driving to Morwell from Traralgon on such a day – the view through the windscreen will become obscured. Many housewives will tell of the settlement of black dust on windowsills and on the washing on the line . . . many people become accustomed to living under such conditions, but there are others who suffer from respiratory troubles, asthmatic conditions and so on who will continue to suffer. It seems that this is the price many will pay in the future as they earn a living in the Latrobe Valley, unless action is taken to remedy the evil.[223]

Although his self-published work was primarily concerned with water pollution and protecting the scenic beauty of the Gippsland Lakes, air pollution and air quality were attendant concerns for Wolfe and other residents of the Valley. Zubrzycki's 1968 study of migrant workers noted that 'grime and soot settle over new paintwork, washing on lines, on goods displayed in shops, and on the green pastures that surround the industrial settlement in the Valley'.[224] Community submissions to the Advance Latrobe Valley Association's newsletter in the 1960s frequently referenced the effects of air pollution, 'verified by any

---

[220] Clifford Ernest Wolfe, *Pollution in the Latrobe Valley and the Gippsland Lakes* (Traralgon: The Author, 1970), 1–2.

[221] Advance Latrobe Valley Association's newsletter, *Powerland*, February 1965.

[222] Zubrzycki, *Settlers of the Latrobe Valley*, 20–22.

[223] Wolfe, *Pollution in the Latrobe Valley and the Gippsland Lakes*, 2.

[224] Zubrzycki, *Settlers of the Latrobe Valley*, 24.

housewife in the area trying to carry out the heartbreaking task of maintaining premises, furnishings and fittings at a reasonable standard of cleanliness'.[225]

In the early post-war period, power plants did not deploy pollution control equipment, which resulted in 'heavy deposition of particulate matter' on the towns of Morwell, Yallourn, and Moe.[226] Air quality monitoring began only in the late 1960s. The installation of newer technology and 'electrostatic precipitators' in the late 1960s removed 'some 90% of particulate matter', but the total load of other pollutants increased dramatically in the 1960s, including the omission of nitrogen oxides, sulphur oxides, and very small particles unable to be captured by electrostatic precipitators. Mortality reports for the Latrobe Valley for the years 1969–1973 revealed 'generally high' mortality levels for both 'the Australian-born and foreign-born residents and particularly high for women, with the overseas-born all causes SMR [Standardise Mortality Ratio] at 99 being the highest for any region in the state'.[227] The report written by sociologists Powles and Birrell went on to argue that:

> of the causes possibly related to pollution, lung cancer only shows significant elevation in the case of foreign-born males. This may reflect occupational exposure, as the dirtiest jobs tend to be done by immigrants ... elevated rate for chronic respiratory disease (bronchitis, emphysema and asthma) are suggestive.[228]

The statistics alone indicated that migrant workers were most affected. This history of workplace health and safety is a silent presence in the storyboard depictions of the Valley's industrial workplaces.

Labour historian Erik Eklund explored what implications these dissenting views of care and the power industry mean for industrial heritage management today. He too highlighted the high rate of lung and respiratory diseases among adult males in the Latrobe Valley from the 1960s onwards. Decades later, investigative media reports revealed what was already known to many health experts: that the coal dust was not nearly as damaging as asbestos. Asbestos was used in the construction of power stations (for insulation, gasket materials for piping, in roofing, walls, and other purposes), and in public housing built for migrant workers in Moe and Morwell from the 1950s to the 1970s. In 1979, the unions developed a taskforce to address risks associated with asbestos exposure in the Valley's power stations and attempted to pressure the SECV to initiate better safety measures and restrict

---

[225] J. B. Mulvaney, 'Air Pollution in the Latrobe Valley: Point of View', *Powerland* (Advance Latrobe Valley Association), 1 February 1966.

[226] John Powles and Robert Birrell, *Mortality in Victoria, 1969–1973: With a Supplement on the Latrobe Valley, 1974–1976* (Melbourne: Environmental Research Associates, Department of Sociology, Monash University, 1977), xxi.

[227] Ibid.   [228] Ibid.

daily exposure. In the decades since, union representatives continued to campaign for recognition (and eventually compensation) of asbestos-related issues.

However, attention to the asbestos issue did not gain wide publicity until much later. A 2001 report by the Victorian State Health Department found the Latrobe Valley had the highest rates of mesothelioma and asbestos-related lung cancers of all municipalities in the state. Numbers in the Valley were expected to rise throughout the 2010s and peak in 2020 due to peoples' past exposure to asbestos. As Eklund highlights, these revelations occurred while the region was suffering economically. Former power station workers had the second highest mesothelioma risk in the country, second only to the infamous mines and mills of Wittenoom, Western Australia, which also heavily employed migrant workers in the 1950s.[229] Throughout the early 2000s, former Latrobe Valley power station workers were contracting the disease at a rate seven times higher than the national average.[230] Although asbestos-related disease has mainly afflicted former SECV workers, the community effects have been widespread. The epidemic places a burden on local healthcare services (and translator services). People with asbestos-related lung cancers needed to travel to Melbourne for treatments.[231] Communities in the Valley were painfully attuned to the issue of poor respiratory health well before the 2014 mine fire, and the disastrous 2009 Black Saturday bushfires.

Researchers behind a 2004 report from the University of Melbourne's Centre for the Study of Health & Society interviewed former SECV workers employed from the 1950s onwards, as well as people who had lost relatives through asbestos-related illnesses, and community members involved in asbestos support or advocacy. In this report, former power station workers could not recall ever being warned about the risks of asbestos exposure or receiving protective gear from the SECV: 'workers described feeling exploited, betrayed and cheated by an employer who they believe put them all at unnecessary risk for the sake of higher productivity'.[232] Documentation and verbal accounts reveal that the SECV were warned and knew about the risks of daily asbestos exposure from the 1940s. The SECV never explicitly acknowledged responsibility for knowingly exposing its workforce to asbestos, although some victims and their families have received monetary compensation. In November 2008, the Victorian government led by Labor Premier John Brumby delivered an apology to asbestos victims and their families in the Valley during a ceremony at

---

[229] Hannah H. Walker and Anthony D. LaMontagne, *Work and Health in the Latrobe Valley: Community Perspectives on Asbestos Issues: Final Report* (Melbourne: Centre for the Study of Health and Society, University of Melbourne, 2004), 3.

[230] Ibid.

[231] Susa Lee, *A Very Public Death: Dying of Mesothelioma and Asbestos Related Lung Cancer in the Latrobe Valley* (Melbourne: Monash University, 2008).

[232] Ibid., 27.

Morwell's Centenary Rose Garden. As the 2008 report stressed, however, compensation and apology did not abate the anger and betrayal felt by former SECV employees and the wider Valley community.

The Park was conceived of and constructed in the thick of these emotions. In the Park, state-backed industry is depicted as reliant on migrant labour; the focal point of this story becomes those labouring people. Plaque six shows groups of coal miners with immigrant backgrounds emerging from a mine shaft, operating a power borer, and breaking for lunch. The images at the Park are concerned not only with an industrial past, but also a working-class past; they are centred on working migrant peoples undertaking physical labour in heavy industry. Herein lies the counterpoint to the seemingly relentless negativity and victimhood I've explored in the previous paragraphs: an active and future-facing nostalgic memory can be effective if it is based on the past actions of wilful subjects. Representations of the worker's body, as agentic even within the structural constraints of the power industry, agentic despite the official rejection of their claims, become important to the politics of recognition in the heritage land-scape. Such representations are interjections into public histories, propelled by knowing subjects and their sense of social justice. As histories of the labour movement have shown, these bodies, especially martyred bodies, can become points of mobilisation for better work conditions and a voice to power.[233]

In summary, my reading resists approaching the storyboard plaques as 'fetishized sites of the state' or a monument to the state-backed coal industry.[234] Rather, they are approached as springboards for telling histories that act as testament to the communal strength of memories around building a life despite adverse structural circumstances and unsafe workplaces. The dissonance in these depictions – that while 'coal may be king', power stations kill people – gets to the heart of heritage debates in the region, and the ambivalence around industrial remains. Dissonance is tied up with the long-term sense of abandonment and powerlessness felt by the Valley population. It is inextricably linked to ideas of care and hospitality, especially that shown towards working-class and migrant peoples. Accordingly, this is an intangible heritage of loss as well as industrial action and resistance.

Privatisation and Demise, 1990s Onwards

Loss is also linked to emotions associated with widespread retrenchment and unemployment in the Valley from the 1990s. In 1980, no one foresaw this scenario.

---

[233] See Zangalis, *Migrant Workers & Ethnic Communities.*

[234] Michael Rothberg, *Multidirectional Memory: Remembering the Holocaust in the Age of Decolonization* (Palo Alto: Stanford University Press, 2009), 20.

Figure 17 Plaque six, again mine workers (photo taken by the author)

A 1980 SECV report proposed to construct twenty-one new power stations in the Gippsland region within the next fifty years in order to meet expected electricity demand.[235] In 1987, they revised their estimates and promoted 'medium-growth' instead. The construction of the Loy Yang power station in the late 1980s had placed the SECV in debt too. By then, the 'major rationalisation programme' overseen by Liberal Jeff Kennett's Victorian government had begun. The process of privatising the SECV's assets quickly resulted in job losses.

Throughout the 1990s, the Kennett government sold various mines and power stations in the Latrobe Valley to international energy companies. The Valley suffered over 5,000 direct job losses over the 1990s as a result, which was about one-third of the population of Morwell. Tens of thousands more job losses followed. Intergenerational employment in one of the Latrobe Valley's large brown coal power stations was common; consequently, the impact on communities of privatisation and successive plant closures has been devastating.[236] Within a couple decades, the Latrobe Valley had the highest rates of unemployment in the state. Even by 2018, the Latrobe Valley had an unemployment rate of 8.2 per cent, the highest in Victoria.[237]

Journalist Tom Doig links the history of privatisation to the unsafe workplace created at Hazelwood in the lead up to the disastrous 2014 mine fire. This fire within Hazelwood coal mine burned for over a month, covering Morwell in toxic smoke and ash. In the wake of privatisation, maintenance jobs at Hazelwood were cut, and this included staff responsible for fire prevention in the open-cut coal mine. From the early 2000s, power stations no longer had a large workforce on call in the event of an emergency (those who were called on in the 1977 mine fire, which raged for three days).[238] CFMEU's Luke van der Meulen put it most bluntly when he stated: 'It's right to say that privatisation is responsible for the extent of that fire.'[239] However, mine fires, especially the 2014 one, are also indicative of long-term issues with workplace health and safety at power stations in the Latrobe Valley, a situation that the workforce has challenged and attempted to remedy through their complaints.

Like Don Fabrizio, Donat Santowiak (introduced in the previous section) also went on to work in heavy industry in the Latrobe Valley. Although he just missed the 'golden age' of full and ongoing employment at the SECV (1940s to 1970s), he recalls the contract and transient nature of his work with

---

[235] Legg, *Heart of the Valley*, 310.
[236] Anna Watanabe, 'What Happens When a Town's Major Industry Shuts Down?' *Insight SBS*, 20 February 2017, www.sbs.com.au/news/insight/article/2017/02/20/what-happens-when-towns-major-industry-shuts-down
[237] Ibid.   [238] Doig, *Hazelwood*, 54.   [239] Cited in Ibid., 54.

fondness, and proceeds to provide a positive spin on the privatisation of the company:

> You know, one minute I could be doing a job in the Yallourn open-cut mine –
> on a dredger – and then the next week I could be at the Hazelwood Power
> Station doing some pressure piping on a boiler. Or then the week after in the
> central workshops in Yallourn redesigning a lathe or something. It was just
> great. You know, it was great. I was offered – early in my traineeship – a nine-
> month stint in the central workshops and I was put through all the different
> trades, actually made things. . . . Yeah it was wonderful. You know, the SEC's
> been criticised for many things but they really had the most wonderful
> upbringing programs for trainees, engineers, and tradespeople. And that's
> proven because nearly everybody's just – you know, since it's all been
> privatised and they all moved on – they're all kicking goals somewhere,
> you know.[240]

Here Donat deals in his own way with the trauma associated with privatisation in the Latrobe Valley. His account also touches on the loss of this type of labouring working class, and the emergence of new (and fewer) higher-paid contract and casualised labourers with specialised skills associated with emerging technologies that displaced other labourers. He is also participating in the common glorification of the SECV, a feature of Doig's journalistic work on the Hazelwood mine fire of 2014 too. Donat ultimately sought work outside the power industry. He took up employment with migrant welfare agencies in West Sale, 65 km north-east from Morwell. He saw this employment move as a natural transition. His comments on funding cuts to ethnic-specific social services under the conservative Liberal Howard government from 1996 mirrors, on a larger scale, the sociopolitical processes that were also inflicting damage to the social fabric of the Latrobe Valley at the time.

2014 Hazelwood Mine Fire

The 2014 mine fire had immediate and long-term health impacts on the community, adding to long-held anxieties over respiratory health in the region. However, this was acknowledged by the state only after protests were organised by community members, especially the 'Voices of the Valley' (VotV) group, led by Morwell local Wendy Farmer. The VotV maintain an active community presence and advocate on behalf of the health and well-being needs of the Latrobe Valley community. Their testimony demonstrates how pivotal they were in reopening the Hazelwood Mine Fire Inquiry (2015–16, Vol 1–4). They successfully campaigned to expand the Inquiry's terms of reference to

---

[240] Santowiak interviewed by Thomson.

include consideration of the rates of deaths as a result of the fire, long-term health issues, and mine rehabilitation:

> We have gathered as much information as we could, tried to make sense of it, and handed all our collected information into the inquiries because the health department wouldn't listen to the people. It turns out that the health department had a 'vested interest' in this information not being made public as they would then be culpable for not taking better care of the community, who knew hey? well just about everyone down here.[241]

The community data they gathered and the subsequent report they submitted to the Inquiry concluded by drawing attention to the deleterious effects of privatisation, and the need for health regulations in the future: 'This mine fire was an industrial spill on a massive scale, not a natural disaster. Our cities are surrounded by privatised mines that the government regulates. We are asking that they are made safe for our health and our children's health.'[242] Groups like the VotV, continue to mount grassroots campaigns against government-backed industry. As this work goes to print, VotV are fighting new proposals to erect a lead smelter in the Valley, a continuation of a much longer history of resistance to industrial and state-backed negligence of local health.

The Valley's ageing migrant population was especially affected by the mine fire. Those with breathing conditions, and the elderly, were encouraged to vacate Morwell. A small one-off payment from the government of $500 per family was provided to those who lived close to the mine. Age care facilities in Morwell, which house a large proportion of Maltese-, Italian-, and Dutch-speaking residents, were shut down and residents were moved out of the Valley. Community reporting also revealed that long-term migrant communities in Morwell took to the streets in protest, directing their animosity to the company GDF Suez, which owned Hazelwood, and the state government, which insisted their health was not at risk despite the evidence.[243] Research released in 2021 expressed concern over atmospheric mercury in the Latrobe Valley. Time-dependant analysis related to the influence of particulate matter on mortality in the wake of Hazelwood's mine fire is only now emerging.[244]

---

[241] Voices of the Valley Inc., www.votv.org.au/about

[242] Voices of the Valley Inc., 'Research Overview, Community Health', October 2014, https://d3n8a8pro7vhmx.cloudfront.net/voicesofthevalley/pages/1/attachments/original/1412945862/VOTV-research-overview-Oct2014.pdf?1412945862

[243] Maltese Community Council of Victoria, 'Disused Open-Pit Coal Mine on Fire in Morwell Causing Havoc in Residents' Lives', 8 March 2014, https://mccv.org.au/news/disused-open-pit-coal-mine-fire-morwell-causing-havoc-residents-lives/

[244] Christina Dimitriadis, Caroline X. Gao, Jillian F. Ikin et al., 'Exposure to Mine Fire Related Particulate Matter and Mortality: A Time Series Analysis from the Hazelwood Health Study', *Chemosphere* 285 (2021): 131351.

Figure 18 Hazelwood coal power station before its demolition in 2020 (photo taken on 30 March 2015 by John Englart, under creative commons, https://images.app.goo.gl/PdTzF7EEsbZMSZrZ7)

Demolition of Industrial Structures and Remembering Industrial Pasts

Fresh memories of the disaster at Hazelwood mine and its public health effects contributed to the mixed emotions around the demolition of the power station in 2020. While public statements from VotV indicate a reluctance to connect the mine fire with the increased incidence of bushfires due to climate change, responses to Hazelwood's demolition demonstrate a growing acceptance in regional Australia that economies need to 'transition' away from coal.[245] This realisation occurs alongside communities' uses of the Park as a space of celebration, pride, and remembrance of migrants' role in industrial labour.

Environment Victoria has campaigned for the transition from coal to clean energy since the 1970s, but in more recent years, public forum discussions and local council publications have also spoken positively about transitioning away from coal.[246] The state-funded Latrobe Valley Energy and Growth Program has

---

[245] John Wiseman, Stephanie Campbell, and Fergus Green, 'Prospects for a "Just Transition" Away from Coal-Fired Power Generation in Australia: Learning from the Closure of the Hazelwood Power Station', CCEP Working Paper 1708, Australian National University, November 2017.

[246] Environment Victoria, 'Safe Climate: Replace Hazelwood', 2017, https://environmentvictoria.org.au/campaign/replace-hazelwood

dedicated $3 million in grants to renewable energy initiatives. Environment Protection Authority Victoria (EPA) began reviewing the operating licences for the Latrobe Valley's three brown coal-fired power stations in November 2017, but the review has yet to be released. Environmental groups are hopeful it will include new restrictions on emissions and air quality monitoring requirements for the region's remaining power stations. Despite the ambivalent situation, historians Eklund and Holm agree that the series of events beginning with the 2014 mine fire and leading to the 2017 closure of Hazelwood and then Morwell power stations 'proved to be the Valley's tipping point for a future without brown coal generation'.[247]

But the path forward for those in favour of energy transition remains unclear. Despite the slow promotion of renewable energy options, the future of coal remains a politically contested issue across the whole country. The context in the Valley is heated and emotive, especially for generations of families who worked in the power industry and still feel left behind by privatisation. The Park for these people becomes a nostalgic oasis in a disappearing industrial landscape. Older retired migrant workers spoke to me with dismay about their children and grandchildren: the youth who cannot find work in the Valley and choose to move away to urban centres like Melbourne. This population loss feeds into a broader community feeling that the state neglects the region.[248] Trade unions and power station officials fear the proposed EPA restrictions will render all plants in the Valley economically unviable, and inflict further damage on the local economy and employment prospects.

Climate change activists have targeted Hazelwood power station and its open-cut mine, depicted numerous times on the Park's storyboard plaques, since at least the 1970s. Protesters and other commentators have dubbed it Australia's 'dirtiest' power station. In 2020, when Hazelwood began to be demolished, it was 54 years old, one of the oldest power stations in the Valley. Local residents uploaded video footage to social media of the demolition of Hazelwood's eight chimneys on 25 May 2020. They did so again in October, when the four dredgers were demolished, and again in December, when the sounds of controlled explosions of Boiler House no. 1 reached residents in Morwell and beyond. Most of the words that accompanied these videos, on Twitter and on Facebook, relished in the demolition of Hazelwood. Nevertheless, this is not an uncontested space. As indicated previously, the

---

[247] Antoinette Holm and Erik Eklund, 'A Post-Carbon Future? Narratives of Change and Identity in the Latrobe Valley, Australia', *BIOS – Zeitschrift für Biographieforschung, Oral History und Lebensverlaufsanalysen*, 31, no. 2 (2020): 13–14.

[248] Jarrod Whittaker, 'Latrobe Valley Population Numbers Fall after Privatisation of Victorian Power Industry', *ABC Gippsland*, 15 April 2019.

destruction of industrial remains is not favoured by all in the Latrobe Valley. Posts about the demolition of Hazelwood made on the 'Gippsland History' Facebook group became heated, with moderators closing comments and stating that 'it was not possible to have a reasoned and respectful discussion on this subject. ... The towers and power stations mean many things to many people. Let us respect that, take time to remember those who wish to, but not add to the pain for those who are hurting'.[249]

The emotions of loss and hurt, and the desire to conserve, also played out a few years earlier over another matter related to the Valley's industrial heritage. In February 2018, the Victorian Heritage Council decided to include the Morwell power station and briquette factory on the Victorian Heritage Register, after local resident Cheryl Wragg made an application. This decision surprised those who had unsuccessfully advocated for preserving Yallourn power stations from demolition in the mid-1990s. However, only a few months after the listing, the Morwell power station was earmarked for demolition, a decision approved by Heritage Victoria, who granted the demolition permit. They did so on the condition site liquidator Energy Brix Australia (EBAC) would develop a Conservation Management Plan. Wragg, angry about this decision, sought legal advice. She also took her opposition to the local media: 'Ms Wragg described EBAC's offer to provide oral histories from former workers and a 3D recording and modelling of the entire site as a "sick joke".'[250]

Despite the community support this media coverage garnered from former power station workers, parts of Morwell power station were demolished from May 2019. EBAC project managers claimed that the conservation of the buildings 'made no economic sense', and that Morwell power station was 'not in a good condition'. The safety issues made the place untenable as a future heritage attraction – not that other heritage advocates and community groups in the region had ever indicated they were interested in developing an industrial heritage hub akin to the Big Pit National Coal Museum in Blaenavon Wales, or the Zollverein Coal Mine Industrial Complex in the Ruhr Valley in West Germany. The Gippsland Immigration Park is the closest Morwell has come to permanent and public commemoration of the region's industrial past. For her part, when the Victorian Heritage Council included the Morwell power station and briquette factory on the Victorian Heritage Register in 2018, Wragg had called it 'the first step in creating an industrial heritage site of national and international significance', and held hope for it triggering a 'whole new large industrial tourism industry activity in our region'. Her fixation on preserving the

---

[249] 'Gippsland History' Facebook page, 25 May 2020.

[250] Heidi Kraak, 'Heritage Proponent to Seek Legal Advice', *Latrobe Valley Express*, 7 June 2018, www.latrobevalleyexpress.com.au/story/5454797/heritage-proponent-to-seek-legal-advice/

physical fabric of industry in an effort to tell the history of power in the region seems to have been misplaced. Historian Erik Eklund, in response to the listing, noted the strong community sentiment that it was the 'wrong choice for the site'.[251] He cited high unemployment and an ageing population as reasons why the region may not be ready for the commodification or 'touristification' of the coal industry. The Park does different heritage work in this context, as a counter-monument and contested celebratory space with deeper and alternative subject-ive histories to facilitate.

EBAC claimed that their heritage approach to Morwell power station would be 'world's best practice as far as capturing heritage information without necessarily retaining buildings'.[252] If done sensitively, and with the inclusion of multiple community voices, such an exercise in intangible heritage making can be a valuable resource to a community grappling with the loss of a coal-mining identity, and aid in the search for meaning in layered historical places. Oral and labour historian Lucy Taksa has similarly main-tained that 'the preservation of industry's tangible material culture, without commensurate interpretation of the intangible cultural heritage associated with labor', severs connections between past, present, and future, and elides the links between this heritage and its class politics.[253] This link becomes important in the wider landscape of Australia's heritage and the politics of recognition (or misrecognition) it espouses. The bottom-up political and social engagements of migrants, or non-Anglophone settlers, is a necessary corrective to the exclusivity and limited social justice agendas of existing public history narratives around industrialisation and progress. This missing link – between heritage and class, between the past, present, and future of migrant subjects in that class history – denies the role of migrants, and institutional responses to them, in the class politics of Australia, and the ongoing fight for migrant workers' rights.

I would also argue that bitter memories are enduring; in the Valley they contribute to a deep ambivalence about industrial remains. The recently released crowd-funded documentary *Our Power: The Latrobe Valley, Hazelwood, and Our Energy Future,* featuring a cast of Latrobe Valley locals, Victorian journalists and academics, directly addressed these memories. *Our Power* told of 'the effects of the privatisation in the 1990s, which severely

---

[251] Eklund cited in Heidi Kraak, 'Heritage Decision a Win for Industrial Tourism Vision: Wragg', *Latrobe Valley Express*, 15 February 2018, https://latrobevalleyexpress.com.au/news/2018/02/14/heritage-decision-a-win-for-industrial-tourism-vision-wragg/.

[252] EBAC, cited in Ibid.

[253] Lucy Taksa, 'Remembering and Incorporating Migrant Workers in Australian Industrial Heritage', *Labor: Studies in Working-Class History* 16, no. 1 (2019): 82.

demoralised the community's pride in electricity production. Since 2014 [the Hazelwood coal mine fire], the Latrobe Valley community has been sparked into action and are taking control of their health, community and future'.[254] Like the Park, this example of community activism most clearly demonstrates how parts of the community have mobilised loss and potentially traumatic memories of the industrial past to advocate for a better communal future for the Valley.

Aside from loss, popular appetite for industrial heritage in the Valley is also tempered by anger, as one respondent wrote in a comment on the Facebook page of the Centre for Gippsland Studies (CGS) (based at Federation University in Churchill):

> The 'debate' in the Latrobe Valley is driven by a history of contempt, disregard and neglect that has been show for the well-being of the residents of the Latrobe Valley by successive federal and state governments, spear headed by the Kennett government. The residents of the LV do not have the luxury to contemplate ideological or academic ideas about history and industrial identity.[255]

The CGS advocate for the protection and conservation of industrial heritage. They bemoan the 'violent process' of large-scale demolition, and its potential psychological and social impacts on the communities of the Valley.[256] Alongside Engineers Australia, they celebrated the saving of Morwell's Dreger no. 9, 'the first true post-war design bucket wheel excavator purchased by the SECV'.[257] It currently rests at the entrance to PowerWorks, an Energy Education centre on the edge of Morwell. PowerWorks was intended to teach school children and tourists about the coal industry. It was shut in 2012 when funding from private energy companies was withdrawn. In 2015, it reopened as a non-for-profit corporation that supported the conservation and display of engineering heritage and aspired to offer 'energy education'. When I visited in early 2020, it was closed. My guide for the day, historian and local Nicolette Snowden, said it had been like that for at least a year. As an explanation for its inactive status, Eklund points to PowerWorks' reliance on volunteer labour, but also extends this reading to argue that industrial heritage in the Valley has a 'low

---

[254] Our Power Documentary, https://ourpowerdoco.com/our-supporters/

[255] Bernard van Rossum, comment in response to the Centre for Gippsland Studies Facebook post, 15 September 2018, 'These images invite you to consider the impact of the removal of "sites of memory," places have become a part of the everyday in the region', showing photos comparing industrial and post-industrial landscapes (with factories removed).

[256] Centre for Gippsland Studies Facebook post, 25 July 2018.

[257] Engineers Australia, Engineering Heritage Australia Recognition Program, September 2016, p. 9.

to modest profile' at the formal or official level, but a richer life at the informal or vernacular level.[258]

The overwhelming tone of public comments regarding industrial heritage on CGS's social media page are negative. Aside from CGS's academic attempts to contextualise the region's industrial heritage, only a 'loose alliance of heritage activists', including Cheryl Wragg, have advocated for the conservation and interpretation of the Valley's industrial remains.[259] Cheryl Wragg has been a prominent, and often lone, heritage advocate. The Committee members behind the Park have not appeared alongside her, despite their status as memory activists. Wragg's father, George Wragg, was an English migrant who arrived in the Valley in 1956 to take up work as a SECV shop steward; he is mentioned earlier in the Element, in the discussion of the 1977 strike. Her familial past, therefore, is intimately connected to the industrial heritage of the region, like members of the Gippsland Immigration Park Committee. While they have channelled their efforts into new platforms – the making of a monu-memorial in the Gippsland Immigration Park – Wragg has focused on the industrial remains, and the nostalgia associated with the SECV 'jobs for life' moniker. Nostalgia for the 'glory days'[260] of the 1950s and 1960s is still a feature of left-wing retellings of the region's past, including *Our Power*. However, these retellings can only become the basis for a radical nostalgia when they also remember the subjective experiences of diverse workers within the SECV, and when they can tackle too the attendant health and environmental effects of that industry. I see this operating in the same way that aforementioned migrant subjects are able to recall their involvement in collective action, and tap into their anger at the SECV, while at the same time fondly recalling a period of relatively secure employment, in contrast to the present socio-economic situation in the Valley. In this vein, some commentators in the heritage debate on social media are able to imagine a post-industrial landscape without any major tangible heritage. This implies that the emotion of pride (and the nostalgia that comes with it) is attached to work and working-class heritage, which is not mutually exclusive from disdain for industrial remains and the (sometimes dam-aging) structures of big corporations. As Donat himself recognises, it is not incompatible, or an act of cognitive dissonance, to esteem aspects of the SECV employment model – the security of ongoing work for some parts of the work-force – and advocate for a 'greening' of the Latrobe Valley.[261]

[258] Eklund, 'The Agents of Industrial Heritage in the Midst of Structural Transformation of the Latrobe Valley, Australia', 156.

[259] Ibid.

[260] Peter Yacono, 'Our Power: The Latrobe Valley, Hazelwood, and Our Energy Future', *Green Agenda*, 2019, https://greenagenda.org.au/2019/02/our-power-film/

[261] Santowiak interviewed by Thomson.

Conclusion

This section has addressed the complexities of modern memory making for migrant and working-class communities faced with deindustrialisation and the (sometime complicit) destruction of sites of collective memory. The GSC sees archival investment as a way forward:

> We are proposing a much-needed archival repository and cultural asset that would serve the information and heritage needs of the whole of Gippsland including assisting in the key challenge of mine rehabilitation. We developed a mutually beneficial model of operating with existing archives and libraries, we consulted extensively with historical societies and family history groups, and we have considered the precedents both in regional Victoria and overseas.[262]

State funding for public history projects has not been forthcoming. Alternatively, there is much community talk about the challenge of mine rehabilitation and adaptive reuse of disused industrial remains in the Valley; but no model has been agreed upon at the date of writing. This conversation is not the same as that which occurs around energy 'transition', although the issue of funding and environmental impact is relevant to both. Putting the safety and economic issues aside for a moment, the 'adaptive reuse' of industrial remains (which was rejected as an option for the now-demolished Morwell power station, discussed earlier in the Element) can only be successful if it speaks to the intangible labour heritage of the Valley. As this section demonstrates, adaptive reuse would fail as a 'radically nostalgic' project if it simply glorified a paternalistic and sometimes damaging industrial era, and did not also address the structural inequalities and family lives tied up in the fate of the power industry.

---

[262] Centre for Gippsland Studies Facebook post, 31 October 2018.

Postscript

Read in the way I have proposed, a multivocal migrant heritage that centres the migrant subject can play a role in 'claims of political legitimacy in a pragmatic politics of recognition and diversity'.[1] The Gippsland Immigration Park, with its depictions of communal life and migrant workers' agency, can be approached as a platform from which to engage in past struggles for social justice, and the aim of parity in negotiations over the distribution of resources of power. As indicated, however, the limits of this politics of recognition lie in its assimilationist assumptions, in the implied acceptance of the settler-colonial state, and its silence on issues of race and the historical racialisation of peoples colonised by the West. Rather than only approaching the Park as complicit in state multiculturalism and the narrative of migrant Others 'contributing to' a core Anglo-Australian culture (another rendering of an assimilationist politics of recognition), we can also approach it as doing heritage work that extends public dialogue beyond the persistent Australian fantasy of monoculture.

Despite the stymied radical potential of the Park, it potentiates class-conscious histories of the region, showing also that nostalgia need not be reactionary or conservative, and that these histories can contain multitudes and dissonance. The Park centres migrant subjectivity, migrant workers' experiences, and activities in collective action and workplace disputes, a rare example in the Valley of an attempt to link tangible and intangible industrial and labour heritages in a meaningful public space.

The Park was created in 2007, and it adhered to the prevailing discourse of state multiculturalism, especially in its funding applications. But the histories, and most importantly the migrant subjects and the personal pasts to which they refer, are tied up with workers and workplaces of an earlier era – when the politics of recognition meant to challenge structural discrimination in addition to calling for parity of participation and representation. Smith and Campbell remind us that in 'contexts of marginalisation', subjugated groups seek 'to garner empathy and thus forge bonds with the past that are used in affective calls for recognition and respect'.[2] As I've also argued, however, the European migrants behind the establishment of the Gippsland Immigration Park can no longer be thought of as subjugated in Australia; they hold relative positions of privilege, including white privilege, which allows them to weaponise their earlier struggles during settlement to argue that 'they have it easy now' when

---

[1] Smith and Campbell, 'Nostalgia for the Future', 617.   [2] Ibid.

referring to more recent (and differently racialised) arrivals. They have been 'recognised' and integrated into the white-settler state. It follows that this has implications for recognising deeper histories of racial subjugation; but it does not mean empathy is stymied, that migrant-settlers to Australia cannot recognise the benefits they reap from the dispossession of Indigenous lands. A politics of recognition, therefore, is bankrupt if it is historically blind – if the distribution of social resources is not accompanied by a longer historical awareness of colonial exploitation, its ongoing effects, and the need for structural and social reparations.

As this work has also shown, the Park potentiates other histories too. Nostalgia has an important part to play in imagining those histories and the social roles they can play in present struggles. Workers and migrant rights go hand in hand, and the story of post-war immigration cannot be told without reference to workplaces, and with that comes a recognition of the care withheld or offered to, received and disputed by the migrant subject. This work has been a longitudinal study of the Latrobe Valley working lives and enduring communities, an attempt to cover the heritage, history, and political economy of this place, while also considering the popular memories associated with the region and its foundation industry, coal. I hope it works as a localised case study, but one that is best understood as part of an international trend of deindustrialisation, a trend that implicates migrant subjects.

Consequently, to understand the uses to which this history is put, we must grapple with the current politics of multiculturalism and its uses in heritage discourses. I've offered not one but a multitude of approaches across these sections in order to address what is at stake in the way industrial and deindustrialising pasts have been and are contested in public debates about working class and multicultural heritage. Primarily, I have been invested in privileging the migrant subject perspective and exploring the nature and political potential of grassroots challenges to positivist state multiculturalism. Even if you disagree with the way in which I've read the politics and history of the Gippsland Immigration Park – searching in (and sometimes against) the gaps and silences of this community-initiated migrant heritage effort – it is undeniably a platform for shared, sedimented, and entangled community histories of the lived experiences of migrant and working-class peoples.

Bibliography

Advance Latrobe Valley Association. *Powerland* (newsletter), February 1965.

Agamben, Giorgio. *Homo Sacer: Sovereign Power and Bare Life*. Stanford: Stanford University Press, 1998.

Agutter, Karen. 'Displaced Persons and the "Continuum of Mobility in the South Australian Hostel System'. In *On the Wing: Mobility Before and After Emigration to Australia, Visible Immigrants*, Volume 7, edited by Margrette Kleinig and Eric Richards, pp. 136–152. Melbourne: Anchor Books, 2013.

Allen, Kristen. *Greek Families in Hawthorn and Clifton Hill*. Melbourne: General Studies Department, Swinburne College of Technology, 1974.

Amalgamated Metal Workers and Shipwrights' Union (Australia), Victorian State Branch. *The 1977 Latrobe Valley Power Strike*. East Melbourne: Amalgamated Metal Workers and Shipwrights' Union, Victorian State Branch, 1978.

Armstrong, Helen. 'Mapping Migrant Memories: Crossing Cultural Borders', *Journal of the Oral History Association of Australia*, no. 19 (1997): 59–65.

Armstrong, Helen. 'Migrant Heritage Places in Australia', *Historic Environment* 13, no. 2 (1997): 12–23.

Ashton, Paul. '"The Birthplace of Australian Multiculturalism?" Retrospective Commemoration, Participatory Memorialisation and Official Heritage', *International Journal of Heritage Studies* 15, no. 5 (2009): 394.

Ashton, Paul, Paula Hamilton, and Rose E. Searby. *Places of the Heart: Memorials in Australia*. Melbourne: Australian Scholarly Publishing, 2012.

Atkinson-Phillips, Alison. *Survivor Memorials: Remembering Trauma and Loss in Contemporary Australia*. Perth: University of Western Australia Press, 2019.

Auciello, Sergio. 'Author's Interview with the Committee', 7 February 2018.

Australian Heritage Commission. *Ask First: A Guide to Respecting Indigenous Heritage Places and Values*. Canberra: Australian Heritage Commission, 2002.

Australian Heritage Commission and Helen Armstrong. *Migrant Heritage Places in Australia: A Guide – How to Find Your Heritage Places*. Canberra: Commonwealth of Australia, 1995.

Australian Heritage Strategy, Commissioned Essays. Damien Bell and Joy Elley, "Whose Heritage?"' 2011. www.environment.gov.au/heritage/austra lian-heritage-strategy/past-consultation/comissioned-essays

Balint, Ruth. '"To Reunite the Dispersed Family": War, Displacement and Migration in the Tracing Files of the Australian Red Cross', *History Australia* 12, no. 2 (2015): 124–142.

Berger, Stefan and Steven High. '(De-) Industrial Heritage: An Introduction', *Labor* 16, no. 1 (2019): 1–27.

Blunt, Alison. 'Collective Memory and Productive Nostalgia: Anglo-Indian Home-making at McCluskieganj', *Environment and Planning D: Society and Space* 21 (2003): 717–738.

Bonnett, Alastair. *Left in the Past: Radicalism and the Politics of Nostalgia*. London: Bloomsbury, 2010.

Bottomley, Gill and Marie M. de Lepervanche, eds. *Ethnicity, Class, and Gender in Australia*. Sydney: Allen & Unwin, 1984.

Bottomley, Gillian. 'Community and Network in a City'. In *Greeks in Australia*, edited by Charles Price, pp. 112–142. Canberra: Australian National University Press, 1975.

Bruer, Jeremy and John Power. 'The Changing Role of the Department of Immigration'. In *The Politics of Australian Immigration*, edited by James Jupp and Marie Kabala, p. 107. Canberra: Australian Government Publishing Service, 1993.

Byrne, Denis. 'A Critique of Unfeeling Heritage'. In *Intangible Heritage*, edited by Laurajane Smith and Natsuko Akagawa, pp. 229–252. London: Routledge, 2009.

Byrne, Denis, Helen Brayshaw, and Tracy Ireland. *Social Significance: A Discussion Paper*. Sydney: NSW National Parks and Wildlife Service, 2003.

Byrne, Denis and Maria Nugent. *Mapping Attachment: A Spatial Approach to Aboriginal Post-Contact Heritage*. Sydney: Department of Environment and Conservation NSW, 2004.

Clarke, Annie and Chris Johnston. 'Time, Memory, Place and Land: Social Meaning and Heritage Conservation in Australia'. Paper Presented at the Scientific Symposium, ICOMOS 14th General Assembly, Zimbabwe, 2003.

Context Heritage Consultants. 'Latrobe City Heritage Study, Volume 1: Thematic Environmental History, Final Report 20 May 2005', Prepared for Latrobe City Council, 27–29.

Coulthard, Glen Sean. *Red Skin White Masks: Rejecting the Colonial Politics of Recognition*. Minneapolis: University of Minnesota Press, 2014.

Cox, David. 'Greek Boys in Melbourne'. In *Greeks in Australia*, edited by Charles Price, pp. 143–187. Canberra: Australian National University Press, 1975.

Curthoys, Ann. 'An Uneasy Conversation: The Multicultural and the Indigenous'. In *Race, Colour and Identity in Australia and New Zealand*, edited by John Docker and Gerhard Fischer, pp. 21–36. Sydney: University of New South Wales Press, 2000.

Dellios, Alexandra. *Histories of Controversy: Bonegilla Migrant Centre*. Melbourne: Melbourne University, 2017.

Dellios, Alexandra. '"It was Just You and Your Child": Single Migrant Mothers, Generational Storytelling and Australia's Migrant Heritage', *Memory Studies* 13, no. 4 (2020): 586–600.

Dellios, Alexandra. 'Migration Parks and Monuments to Multiculturalism: Finding the Challenge to Australian Heritage Discourses through Community Public History Practice', *The Public Historian* 42, no. 2 (2020): 7–32.

Dellios, Alexandra. 'Remembering Mum and Dad: Family History Making by Children of Eastern European Refugees', *Immigrants and Minorities: 'Special Issue: Memory and Family in Australian Refugee Histories'* 36, no. 2 (2018): 105–124.

Di Fabrizio, Donato. 'Donato Di Fabrizio – Australia'. In *Le 1001 storie degli Italiani nel Mondo*, Edited by Monica Palozzi, p. 150. Athens: Pragmata, 2018.

Dicks, Bella. 'Performing the Hidden Injuries of Class in Coal-Mining Heritage', *Sociology* 42, no. 3 (2008): 436–452.

Doig, Tom. *Hazelwood*. Melbourne: Random House Australia, 2019.

Earle, Samuel. 'The Toxic Nostalgia of Brexit', *The Atlantic*, 5 October 2017, https://www.theatlantic.com/international/archive/2017/10/brexit-britain-may-johnson-eu/542079/.

Edwards, Debbie. *Morwell, a Historical Walk*. Victoria: D. Edwards, 1993.

Eklund, Erik. 'The Agents of Industrial Heritage in the Midst of Structural Transformation of the Latrobe Valley, Australia'. In *Constructing Industrial Pasts: Heritage, Historical Culture and Identity in Regions Undergoing Structural Economic Transformation*, edited by Stefan Berger, pp. 146–159. Oxford, New York: Berghahn Books, 2020.

Eklund, Erik. *Mining Towns: Making a Living, Making a Life*. Sydney: University of New South Wales Press, 2012.

Eklund, Erik. '"There Needs to be Something There for People to Remember": Industrial Heritage in Newcastle and the Hunter Valley, Australia'. In *Industrial Heritage and Regional Identities*, edited by Christian Wicke, Stefan Berger, and Jana Golombek, pp. 168–189. London: Routledge, 2018.

El-Enany, Nadine. *(B)ordering Britain: Law, Race and Empire*. Manchester: Manchester University Press, 2020.

Environment Victoria. 'Safe Climate: Replace Hazelwood'. 2017, https://envir onmentvictoria.org.au/campaign/replace-hazelwood

Erll, Astrid. 'Cultural Memory Studies: An Introduction'. In *A Companion to Cultural Memory Studies*, edited by Ansgar Nunning and Astrid Erll, pp. 1–18. Berlin: De Gruyter, 2010.

Farhall, Kate, Meagan Tyler and Peter Fairbrother. 'Labour and Regional Transition: Sex-Segregation, the Absence of Gender and the Valorisation of Masculinised Employment in Gippsland, Australia', *Gender, Place & Culture* 28, no. 12 (2021): 1755–1777.

Fitzroy Ecumenical Centre, Quarterly Journal *EKSTASIS*, No. 8, February 1974.

Fletcher, Meredith. *Digging People Up for Coal: A History of Yallourn.* Melbourne: Melbourne University Publishing, 2002.

Fraser, Nancy. 'From Redistribution to Recognition? Dilemmas of Justice in a "Post-Socialist" Age', *New Left Review* I/211 (July 1995).

Fraser, Nancy. 'Progressive Neoliberalism versus Reactionary Populism: A Choice that Feminists should Refuse', *Nordic Journal of Feminist and Gender Research* 24, no. 4 (2016): 281–284.

Fraser, Nancy. 'Social Justice in the Knowledge Society: Redistribution, Recognition, and Participation', *Heinrich Boll Stiftung* 5 (2001): 1–13.

Frisch, Michael. *A Shared Authority: Essays on the Craft and Meaning of Oral and Public History.* New York: State University of New York Press, 1990.

Fuel for Unrest: People, Power and Planning in the Latrobe Valley. Melbourne: Brown Coal Study Group, Conservation Council of Victoria, 1981.

Gest, Justin. *The New Minority: White Working Class Politics in an Age of Immigration and Inequality.* Oxford: Oxford University Press, 2016.

Gilroy, Paul. *There Ain't No Black in the Union Jack: The Cultural Politics of Race and Nation.* London: Hutchinson, 1987.

Gippsland Immigration Park Committee. 'Gippsland Immigration Wall of Recognition: Souvenir Booklet – Official Opening, March 18th 2007', 2007.

Gippsland Immigration Park Committee response to initial survey. 'Personal Correspondence', 4 August 2017.

Gnecco, Christobal. 'Heritage in Multicultural Times'. In *The Palgrave Handbook of Contemporary Heritage Research*, edited by Emma Waterton and Steve Watson, pp. 263–280. London: Palgrave Macmillan, 2015.

Golding, Viv and Wayne Modest, eds. *Museums and Communities: Curators, Collections and Collaboration.* London: Bloomsbury, 2013.

Gunaikurnai Land and Water Aboriginal Corporation. 'Annual Report 2019'. https://gunaikurnai.org.au/wp-content/uploads/2019/12/GLaWAC-Annual-Report-2019-WEB-FINAL.pdf

Gunew, Sneja. *Haunted Nations: The Colonial Dimensions of Multiculturalisms*. London: Routledge, 2013.

Hage, Ghassan. *White Nation: Fantasies of White Supremacy in a Multicultural Society*. London: Routledge, 2012.

Hall, Catherine. 'Doing Reparatory History: Bringing "Race" and Slavery Home', *Race & Class* 60, no. 1 (2018): 3–21.

Hall, Stuart. *Fateful Triangle: Race, Ethnicity, Nation*, edited by Kobena Mercer. Cambridge, MA: Harvard University Press, 2017.

Hellings, Stephen. *Footsteps through Time: A Heritage Walk Depicting the Morwell of Yester-Year*. Morwell: Morwell Historical Society, 2001.

Hellings, Stephen. *Heritage Fact File: A Brief Look at Some Dates Names and Events*. Morwell: Morwell Historical Society, 2001.

Hellings, Stephen. *Morwell: Memories and Milestones*. Morwell: Morwell Historical Society, 1999.

Hirsch, Marianne. 'Stateless Memory', *Critical Times* 2, no. 3 (2019): 416–434.

Hirst, John. *Sense and Nonsense in Australian History*. Melbourne: Black Inc., 2009.

Hobbins, Peter, Ursula Frederick, and Anne Clarke. *Stories from the Sandstone: Quarantine Inscriptions from Australia's Immigrant Past*. Sydney: Arbon, 2017.

Isaacs, Eva. *Greek Children in Sydney*. Canberra: Australian National University Press, 1976.

Jakubowicz, Andrew. 'The Realities of Australian Multiculturalism'. In *'For Those Who've Come Across the Seas ... ': Australian Multicultural Theory, Policy and Practice*, edited by Andrew Jakubowicz and Christina Ho, pp. 3–14. Melbourne: Australian Scholarly Publishing, 2013.

Jarvis, Helen and Alastair Bonnett. 'Progressive Nostalgia in Novel Living Arrangements: A Counterpoint to Neo-traditional New Urbanism?' *Urban Studies* 50, no. 11 (2013): 2349–2370.

Johnston, Chris and Australian Heritage Commission. *What is Social Value? A Discussion Paper*. Canberra: Australian Government Publishing Service, 1992.

Jupp, James. *From White Australia to Woomera: The Story of Australian Immigration*. London: Cambridge University Press, 2002.

Keightley, Emily and Michael Pickering. *The Mnemonic Imagination: Remembering as Creative Practice*. London: Palgrave Macmillan, 2012.

Kirshenblatt-Gimblett, Barbara. 'Intangible Heritage as Metacultural Production', *Museum International* 56, no. 1–2 (2004): 163–174.

Klein, Kerwin Lee. 'On the Emergence of Memory in Historical Discourse', *Representations* 69 (2000): 127–150.

Kraak, Heidi. 'Heritage Proponent to Seek Legal Advice', *Latrobe Valley Express*, 7 June 2018. www.latrobevalleyexpress.com.au/story/5454797/heritage-proponent-to-seek-legal-advice/

Kunz, Egon. *Displaced Persons: Calwell's New Australians*. Canberra: Australian National University Press, 1988.

Lake, Marilyn and Henry Reynolds. *Drawing the Global Colour Line: White Men's Countries and the Question of Racial Equality*. Melbourne: Melbourne University Publishing, 2008.

Langmore, Dacud. *Planning Power: The Uses and Abuses of Power in the Planning of the Latrobe Valley*. Melbourne: Australian Scholarly Publishing, 2013.

Latrobe City Council. 'Latrobe Planning Scheme Planning Scheme Review Report', April 2008. www.latrobe.vic.gov.au/sites/default/files/Latrobe_Planning_Scheme_Review_Report_April_2008.pdf

Lee, Susa. *A Very Public Death: Dying of Mesothelioma and Asbestos Related Lung Cancer in the Latrobe Valley*. Melbourne: Monash University, 2008.

Legg, Stephen Mark. *Heart of the Valley: A History of the Morwell Municipality*. Melbourne: Royal Victorian Institute for the Blind, 1995.

Little, Barbara and Paul Shackel. *Archaeology, Heritage, and Civic Engagement: Working Toward the Public Good*. London: Routledge, 2016.

Littler, Jo and Roshi Naidoo, eds. *The Politics of Heritage: The Legacies of Race*. London: Routledge, 2004.

Littler, Jo and Roshi Naidoo. 'White Past, Multicultural Present: Heritage and National Stories'. *Cultural Heritage: Critical Concepts in Media and Cultural Studies*, Volume 11, edited by Laurajane Smith, pp. 101–113. Oxon: Routledge, 2006.

Lixinski, Lucas. 'Selecting Heritage: The Interplay of Art, Politics and Identity', *European Journal of International Law* 22, no. 1 (2011): 81–100.

Lloyd, Sarah and Julie Moore. 'Sedimented Histories: Connections, Collaborations and Co-production in Regional History', *History Workshop Journal* 80, no. 1 (2015): 234–248.

Lopez, Mark. *The Origins of Multiculturalism in Australian Politics, 1945–1975*. Melbourne: Melbourne University Press, 2000.

Maltese Community Council of Victoria. 'Disused Open-Pit Coal Mine on Fire in Morwell Causing Havoc in Residents' Lives', 8 March 2014. https://mccv.org.au/news/disused-open-pit-coal-mine-fire-morwell-causing-havoc-residents-lives/

Marr, David. 'The White Queen: One Nation and the Politics of Race', *Quarterly Essay* 65 (2017): 1–102.

Martin, Jean. *The Migrant Presence: Australian Responses, 1947–1977.* Sydney: George Allen and Unwin, 1978.

McDonald, Brooke, Sandy Gifford, Kim Webster, John Wiseman, and Sue Casey. *Refugee Resettlement in Regional and Rural Victoria: Impacts and Policy Issues.* Melbourne: Victorian Health Promotion Foundation and prepared by the Refugee Health Research Centre, La Trobe University, 2008. https://refugeehealthnetwork.org.au/wp-con tent/uploads/RefugeeResettlement_Web_Vichealth+report.pdf

McShane, Ian. 'Challenging or Conventional? Migration History in Australian Museums'. In *Negotiating Histories: National Museums Conference Proceedings*, edited by Darryl McIntyre and Kirsten Wehner, pp. 122–133. Canberra: National Museum of Australia, 2001.

Mercer, Patrick. 'Australia's Double Standard on Statues and Sacred Sites', *Kill Your Darlings*, 30 August 2020. www.killyourdarlings.com.au/article/austra lias-double-standard-on-statues-and-sacred-sites/

Modood, Tariq. *Multiculturalism.* Cambridge: Polity Press, 2013.

Monument Australia. 'Angus McMillan Expedition'. 2010–2022, http://monu mentaustralia.org.a0075/themes/landscape/exploration/display/30535- angus-mcmillan-expedition

Morgan, Patrick. 'Gippsland Settlers and the Kurnai Dead', *Quadrant* 48, no. 10 (2004): 26–28.

Mulvaney, J. B. 'Air Pollution in the Latrobe Valley: Point of View', *Powerland* (Advance Latrobe Valley Association), 1 February 1966.

Munjeri, Dawson. 'Tangible and Intangible Heritage: From Difference to Convergence', *Museum International* 56, no. 1–2 (2004): 12–20

National Archives of Australia (NAA), A445, 276/2/4. 'Unemployed Migrants: Confidential Report', *Hazel Dobson to the Secretary for the Department of Immigration*, 14 May 1952.

Nicolacopoulos, Toula and George Vassilacopoulos. 'On the Methodology of Greek-Australian Historiography'. In *Greek Research in Australia: Proceedings of the Biennial International Conference of Greek Studies*, edited by Elizabeth Close, Michael Tsianikas, and George Frazis. Adelaide: Flinders University, 2005.

Norton, Claire and Mark Donnelly. *Liberating Histories.* London: Routledge, 2018.

Novoa, Magdalena. 'Gendered Nostalgia: Grassroots Heritage Tourism and (De)industrialization in Lota, Chile', *Journal of Heritage Tourism* (2021): 1–19.

Nugent, Maria. 'Mapping Memories: Oral History for Aboriginal Cultural Heritage in New South Wales, Australia'. In *Oral History and Public*

Memories, edited by Paula Hamilton and Linda Shopes, pp. 47–63. Philadelphia: Temple University Press, 2008.

O'Dowd, Liam. 'From a "Borderless World" to a "World of Borders": "Bringing History Back in"', *Environment and Planning D: Society & Space* 28, no. 6 (2010): 1031–1050.

Our Power Documentary. 2019, https://ourpowerdoco.com/our-supporters/

Paton, Aunty Doris, Jessica Horton, and Beth Marsden. 'Telling the Truth about Gippsland's History', *Overland*, 6 October 2020. https://overland.org.au/2020/10/telling-the-truth-about-gippslands-history

Pfoser, Alena. 'Memory and Everyday Borderwork: Understanding Border temporalities', *Geopolitics* (2020): 1–18.

Poria, Yaniv, Richard Butler, and David Airey. 'The Core of Heritage Tourism', *Annals of Tourism Research* 30, no. 1 (2003): 238–254.

Powles, John and Robert Birrell. *Mortality in Victoria, 1969–1973: With a Supplement on the Latrobe Valley, 1974–1976*. Melbourne: Environmental Research Associates, Department of Sociology, Monash University, 1977.

Project Management Group. 'Author's Interview with the Committee', 7 February 2018.

Reeves, Keir, Erik Eklund, Andrew Reeves, Bruce Scates, and Vicki Peel. 'Broken Hill: Rethinking the International Significance of the Material Culture and Intangible Heritage of the Australian Labour Movement', *International Journal of Heritage Studies* 17, no. 4 (2011): 301–317.

Richards, Eric. *Destination Australia: Migration to Australia since 1901*. Sydney: University of New South Wales Press, 2008.

Rothberg, Michael. *Multidirectional Memory: Remembering the Holocaust in the Age of Decolonization*. Palo Alto: Stanford University Press, 2009.

Santowiak, Donat Interviewed by Alistair Thomson in the Australian Generations Oral History Project, National Library of Australia, 2014. https://nla.gov.au/nla.obj-220175608/listen

Simic, Zora. 'Bachelors of Misery and Proxy Brides: Marriage, Migration and Assimilation, 1947–1973', *History Australia* 11, no. 1 (2014): 149–174.

Smith, Laurajane. *Emotional Heritage: Visitor Engagement at Museums and Heritage Sites*. London: Routledge, 2021.

Smith, Laurajane. *Uses of Heritage*. London: Routledge, 2006.

Smith, Laurajane. '"We are . . . We are Everything": The Politics of Recognition and Misrecognition at Immigration Museums', *Museum and Society* 15, no. 1 (2017): 69–86.

Smith, Laurajane and Emma Waterton. *Heritage, Communities and Archaeology*. London: Bloomsbury Academic, 2013.

Smith, Laurajane and Gary Campbell. '"Nostalgia for the Future": Memory, Nostalgia and the Politics of Class', *International Journal of Heritage Studies* 23, no. 7 (2017): 615.

Smith, Laurajane, Margaret Wetherell, and Gary Campbell. *Emotion, Affective Practices and the Past in the Present*. London: Routledge, 2018.

Solidarity. 'Latrobe Valley 1977 Power Strike', 8 September 2017. www.soli darity.net.au/unions/latrobe-valleys-1977-power-strike/

Spearritt, Peter. 'Money, Taste and Industrial Heritage', *Australian Historical Studies* 24, no. 96 (1991): 33–45.

State Electricity Commission of Victoria, Country Roads Board. *Central Gippsland Social Survey: A Socio-Economic Study of the Latrobe Valley: A Report*. Melbourne: C. H. Rixon, Government Printer, 1975.

Steel, Kathryn. 'Point of View: A Significant Regional Industrial Dispute from a Novel Perspective', *Provenance: The Journal of Public Record Office Victoria*, no. 12 (2013).

Stevens, Gary. 'The Vision to Succeed', *Latrobe Valley Express*, 28 January 2016.

Storer, Des and Centre for Urban Research & Action, eds. *Ethnic Rights, Power and Participation Toward a Multi-Cultural Australia*. Melbourne: Clearing House on Migration Issues, Ecumenical Migration Centre, and Centre for Urban Research and Action, 1975.

Gippsland Immigration Wall Committee. *Stories from the Gippsland Immigration Wall of Recognition*, Volume 1. Morwell: Gippsland Immigration Park Inc., 2012.

Strangleman, Tim. 'Mining a Productive Seam? The Coal Industry, Community and Sociology', *Contemporary British History* 32, no. 1 (2018): 18–38.

Taksa, Lucy. 'Labor History and Public History in Australia: Allies or Uneasy Bedfellows?' *International Labor and Working-Class History*, no. 76 (2009): 84–85.

Taksa, Lucy. 'Machines and Ghosts: Politics, Industrial Heritage and the History of Working Life at the Eveleigh Workshops', Volume 85. *Labour History* (2003): 65–88.

Taksa, Lucy. 'Remembering and Incorporating Migrant Workers in Australian Industrial Heritage', *Labor: Studies in Working-Class History* 16, no. 1 (2019): 82.

Tavan, Gwenda. *The Long Slow Death of White Australia*. Carlton North: Scribe, 2005.

The Gippsland Institute of Advanced Education to the Town and Country Planning Board, State Electricity Commission of Victoria, Country Roads Board, and Central Gippsland Social Survey, *A Socio-Economic Study of the*

Latrobe Valley: A Report. Melbourne: C. H. Rixon, Government Printer, 1975.

Tsiolkas, Christos. 'Class, Identity, Justice: Reckoning with the Ghosts of Europe', *Griffith Review: The European Exchange* 69 (2020), pp. 17–27.

United Nations Declaration on the Rights of Indigenous Peoples, adopted by the General Assembly in 2007.

Victoria State Government. 'Multicultural Community Infrastructure Fund', 2019–2020. https://content.vic.gov.au/sites/default/files/2019-11/multicul tural-community-infrastructure-fund-2019-2020-guidelines.pdf

Voices of the Valley Inc. 'Research Overview, Community Health', October 2014. https://d3n8a8pro7vhmx.cloudfront.net/voicesofthevalley/pages/1/ attachments/original/1412945862/VOTV-research-overview-Oct2014.pdf? 1412945862

Walker, Hannah and Anthony D. LaMontagne. *Work and Health in the Latrobe Valley: Community Perspectives on Asbestos Issues: Final Report.* Melbourne: Centre for the Study of Health and Society, University of Melbourne, 2004.

Watanabe, Anna. 'What Happens When a Town's Major Industry Shuts Down?' *Insight SBS.* 2019. https://www.sbs.com.au/news/insight/what-happens-when-a-town-s-major-industry-shuts-down

Waterton, Emma and Laurajane Smith. 'The Recognition and Misrecognition of Community Heritage', *International Journal of Heritage Studies* 16, no. 1–2 (2010): 4–15.

Waterton, Emma, Laurajane Smith, and Gary Campbell. 'The Utility of Discourse Analysis to Heritage Studies: The Burra Charter and Social Inclusion', *International Journal of Heritage Studies* 12, no. 4 (2006): 339–355.

Watson, Ian. *A Disappearing World: Case Studies in Class, Gender and Memory.* Melbourne: Scholarly Publishing, 2015.

Whittaker, Jarrod. 'Latrobe Valley Population Numbers Fall after Privatisation of Victorian Power Industry', *ABC Gippsland*, 15 April 2019. https://www .abc.net.au/news/2019-04-15/figures-show-latrobe-valley-youth-popula tion-drop/11000784

Wicke, Christian, Stefan Berger, and Jana Golombek, eds. *Industrial Heritage and Regional Identities.* London: Routledge, 2018.

Williams, Joan. *White Working Class: Overcoming Class Cluelessness in America.* Boston: Harvard Business Review Press, 2017.

Wise, Amanda and Selvaraj Velayutham. 'Introduction: Multiculturalism and Everyday Life'. In *Everyday Multiculturalism*, edited by Amanda Wise and Selvaraj Velayutham. London: Palgrave Macmillan, 2009, pp. 1–17.

Wiseman, John, Stephanie Campbell and Fergus Green. 'Prospects for a "Just Transition" Away from Coal-Fired Power Generation in Australia: Learning from the Closure of the Hazelwood Power Station', CCEP Working Paper 1708, Australian National University, November 2017.

Wolfe, Clifford Ernest. *Pollution in the Latrobe Valley and the Gippsland Lakes*. Traralgon: The Author, 1970.

Yacono, Peter. 'Our Power: The Latrobe Valley, Hazelwood, and Our Energy Future', *Green Agenda*. 2019. https://greenagenda.org.au/2019/02/our-power-film/

York, Barry. 'The Boarding Houses of 1950s Coburg', *Search: The Quarterly Journal of the Coburg Historical Society* no. 121 (December 2020).

Zangalis, George Interviewed by Kristina Kukolja in the Unwanted Australians Oral History Project – ORAL TRC 6920/1, National Library of Australia. 2019.

Zangalis, George. *Migrant Workers & Ethnic Communities: Their Struggles for Social Justice & Cultural Rights: The Role of Greek-Australians*. Melbourne: Common Ground, 2009.

Zangalis, George. 'Our Unions or Theirs'. In *Ethnic Rights, Power and Participation Toward a Multi-Cultural Australia*, edited by Des Storer and Centre for Urban Research & Action. Melbourne: Clearing House on Migration Issues, Ecumenical Migration Centre, and Centre for Urban Research and Action, 1975.

Zubrzycki, Jerzy. *Settlers of the Latrobe Valley: A Sociological Study of Immigrants in the Brown Coal Industry in Australia*. Canberra: Australian National University, 1964.

Cambridge Elements ≡

Critical Heritage Studies

Kristian Kristiansen,
University of Gothenburg

Michael Rowlands,
UCL

Francis Nyamnjoh,
University of Cape Town

Astrid Swenson,
Bath University

Shu-Li Wang,
Academia Sinica

Ola Wetterberg,
University of Gothenburg

About the Series

This series focusses on the recently established field of Critical Heritage Studies. Interdisciplinary in character, it brings together contributions from experts working in a range of fields, including cultural management, anthropology, archaeology, politics, and law. The series will include volumes that demonstrate the impact of contemporary theoretical discourses on heritage found throughout the world, raising awareness of the acute relevance of critically analysing and understanding the way heritage is used today to form new futures.

Cambridge Elements ᐸ

Critical Heritage Studies

Printed in the United States
by Baker & Taylor Publisher Services